MORE BOOKS FROM THE SAGER GROUP

#MeAsWell, A Novel
by Peter Mehlman

The Orphan's Daughter, A Novel
by Jan Cherubin

Meeting Mozart: A Novel Drawn from the Secret Diaries
of Lorenzo Da Ponte
by Howard Jay Smith

The Allergic Boy Versus the Left-Handed Girl: A Novel
by Michael Kun

Eat Wheaties! A Novel
By Michael Kun

Miss Havilland, A Novel
by Gay Daly

Shaman: The Mysterious Life and Impeccable Death
of Carlos Castaneda
by Mike Sager

Lifeboat No. 8: Surviving the Titanic
by Elizabeth Kaye

See our entire library at TheSagerGroup.net

SARABETH
AND THE FIVE
SPIRITS

A Novel
About Channeling,
Consciousness,
Healing and Murder

BY BETH GINERIS

Sarabeth and The Five Spirits: A Novel about Channeling, Consciousness, Healing and Murder

Cover Photo by Bryan Goff on Unsplash.com
Cover and Interior Designed by Siori Kitajima,
SF AppWorks LLC

Cataloging-in-Publication data for this book is available from the Library of Congress
ISBN-13:
eBook: 978-1-950154-56-2
Paperback: 978-1-950154-57-9

Published by The Sager Group LLC
TheSagerGroup.net

SARABETH
AND THE FIVE
SPIRITS

A Novel
*About Channeling,
Consciousness,
Healing and Murder*

BY BETH GINERIS

THE SAGER GROUP

Artifex Te Adiuva

For Kate

CONTENTS

Prologue 1

Chapter 1 5

Chapter 2 17

Chapter 3 31

Chapter 4.. 45

Chapter 5 63

Chapter 6..75

Chapter 7 93

Chapter 8.. 105

Chapter 9..125

Chapter 10 131

Chapter 11.. 159

Chapter 12 171

Chapter 13..195

About the Author..213

About the Publisher 214

PROLOGUE

In an effort to use her Center for Instinctive Health Medicine for the elevation of consciousness, Sarabeth Lewis has developed a program to increase present-moment awareness and sense perception. It was designed to help each person reset his or her understanding of the tapestry of life and promote the creation of life-affirming action on the planet. Sarabeth, along with her husband, Rob Laws, and 12-year-old daughter, Sophia, open their home to others for a weekend of channeled information. Astral-spirit guides from outside the current time-space continuum, planetary constellations, mythical heroes, and ancient cultures all present themselves through Sarabeth as the communication vehicle. This process is called "channeling" and results in an opportunity for these guides to dialogue with the participants in real time.

Sarabeth synthesizes her innate capacity to channel from the collective with her source-embedded sensory guidance system. She focuses the information through her heart center. She connects with these other-dimension spirit beings to gather elevated ideas and practices to increase mindful and peaceful action on the planet. The interconnected body of human, animal, plant, earth, and stars that create life is the integrated tapestry of life she is attempting to correct: Sarabeth has identified that without change, the global community is going to destroy the planet.

Humankind has lost its intuitive communication with nature, which has destabilized the energetic field around the planet. Without the reestablishment of this connection, the planet will not be able to cleanse the negative physical destruction or the energetic debris that is blocking the health of the ecosystem of the integrated tapestry of life. Through her research and her energetic practices, Sarabeth has come to understand the natural push of life identified in ancient spiritual texts across cultures and civilizations: that all life is interconnected in a tapestry of life. There is a unified field of energy, and she feels the urgency to heal the planet now. Her goal for the weekend is to demonstrate and seed the way to follow and inhabit these heart-led connections as a new way and a new path—supported via sensefulness and mindfulness to respond to and maintain the global embedded presence priority.

The action begins with Sarabeth alone communing with her spirit guides in a traditional style of channeling. She has incorporated the highly effective healing tradition of communing directly with nature in addition to channeling in order to keep her frequency of light high.

Her friends begin to arrive after she has completed this opening and the stage is set for the development of the new path toward healing the planet. The goal is to establish information in place from the higher dimensions of reality so that these participants can integrate the new information within their own practice and training, in order to seed their practices with this new, light-filled information. With these few individuals, through the simple introduction of the information, a dramatic shift in consciousness can take place and lead to a shift in the natural course of human and nature interaction to heal the planet on a global level.

Nine-year-old Sarabeth, brown hair waving across her shoulders, puts one foot in front of the other, with a combination of distraction and confidence along a 6-foot-high cinderblock wall. She has made this journey dozens of times. Touching flowers and tree branches along the way, she grabs cherries and buds, eating and smelling as she moves along the wall. Reaching her destination with flowers and

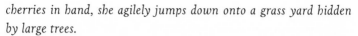

cherries in hand, she agilely jumps down onto a grass yard hidden by large trees.

Sunlight pours into the center of her favorite secret garden space. She immediately steps out of the cool air hanging under the tall trees and looks up into the cerulean blue sky accentuated with white billowing clouds, smiling at the sensation of the sun's rays on her face. She scans for the perfect spot. At once she eyes a bench in the center of a circle of yellow flowers. She sits down on the bench next to a resting dragonfly. She greets the dragonfly from her mind and hears a quiet hello. Looking at each flower and tree, she sends and receives messages.

Her cherries finished, she lays the flower next to her. Absentmindedly, she folds her legs under her, her back aligns her spine, and her arms fall, lightly resting beside her hips. She waits. And then, almost imperceptibly from the corner of her eye, it happens: She sees the web of life grow. Each living entity begins to have an enhanced color or light encircling it. And then, like a laser show, a light emanates from each to the other. Finally, the light points to her from each singular entity and she is centered inside the web of life. She feels the communication from each source like a beautiful song of light.

Trees and flowers, bees and dragonflies, birds, and a squirrel bounding across the grass all speak through her in singular voices. The light continues to grow to include the clouds in the sky. As she allows herself to be filled with the light and the song, her heart swells open to hundreds of webstrings of light and energy connecting her to other areas. She feels the idents to her family, friends, teachers, and pets. Inside her being, she is filled with the unified field of energy and light surrounding the planet. She is hit not only by the beauty but also the pain and sadness of the earth. She is electrified with the feelings and knowings of the plants and beings around her, energized with a sense of oneness. She sits. Her hands are tingling. An intention to offer healing is received. The webstrings sing with light as her being emanates a vibration of healing energy out into the universe.

Hours pass while she is in this trance-state. The cool air on her back awakens her from her reverie. The sun fading behind the tall trees reminds her it is time to return to the mundane. She slowly gets up from the bench. Lightly nodding to the flowers, the trees, and the web of life around her, she climbs up the tree closest to the wall and starts back home.

CHAPTER 1

To understand health through Chinese Medicine, discern The Three Treasures: Shen (spirit), Qi (energy), and Jing (life essence), and The Five Constituents: Shen, Qi (moisture), Blood, and Essence (Jing), which exist on a lesser to greater density and materiality. Shen is ephemeral, spirit/mind, and lacking in substantiality. Shen and Jing work together, integrated mind/body/spirit or psyche/soma, to form the blueprint and life force of a person. Shen, Qi, and Jing maintain shape, function, and identity (what is), and through these the self-making, self-transforming, and self-actualizing human capacity.

"Qi (energy, mind, or thoughts) follow Shen (spirit), and Blood (physical body) follows Qi (energy) (mind)." This is the theory that thoughts create your destiny; that what you believe you see.

Qi is insubstantial and unseen and follows Shen. It is more substantial than Shen but less substantial than moisture, and lesser than blood. Qi and Blood maintain the body's form and composition, incorporating moisture, the body's fluid (Jin ye). Qi is more dynamic and changeable than blood (Xue). Blood is more stable and denser. As disease moves from Shen to Qi to Blood it becomes more solid and less moveable. Jing is the most intractable and has the greatest density.

These define the human body. A harmonious, balanced relationship between these results in health; an unbalanced, disharmonious interaction between these results in disease. This relationship flows in both directions. Healing can occur from density to insubstantial and from the most insubstantial to most dense; thus shifting thinking, seeing, and perception allows for what appear to be miracles of transformation.

—Fundamentals of Chinese Medical Theory & Practice, 2nd century BCE

Sarabeth sits on her beige couch with her legs crossed under her. She is alone in her study. It's 3 o'clock in the afternoon—her favorite time of the day, when the sun streams in on the egg-yolk yellow walls and makes them vibrate in golden light. Tibetan bowls sing a monotonous, mesmerizing hum in the background. Leo, sleeping at her feet, is lightly crying in his dream. She reaches down and pats him, saying, "You're OK." He opens his eye, absently licks her hand, and falls back asleep. Sarabeth closes her eyes, repositions herself in a half lotus position with her hands gently held in her lap, takes a cough drop and puts it into her mouth. She begins her opening meditation, anchoring in language her intention for the retreat she is about to lead at the hacienda, which was once her parents' home. As she recedes into the meditative space, sweet and melancholy experiences rapidly present and fill her heart. With an inner refocus she brushes these memories aside and begins her opening mantra:

"Dear god, goddess, and great spirit: Allow me to be a clear healing channel. I would like to call in a hundred thousand angels to please come in and fill this room and surround this space. I call in only high light beings to guide me and offer me interpretation for this weeklong retreat on healing psycho-emotional trauma through the ancient traditions. Thank you for your protection and guidance dear Archangel Michael, Metatron, and Sirius, Orion, the Council of Twelve, and the Marys… "

Sarabeth feels the voice and words from the channel and begins to simply speak what is presented to her. Her voice lightens and deepens, gaining increased softness as she speaks the words as if they are her own. She instantly knows the content even as she herself hears them from her own voice for the first time:

"Dearly beloved, we are here and want you to know we are grateful for your work in upleveling the light on the planet. This weekend is about bringing increased light into the vessels of the participants—you have several high-power beings at the conference ready to *integrate these healing traditions. All is energy and light. Love is the best emotion on which to focus your attention and is the most healing response. Acceptance, allowing, and love—through this you will open the door for initiates to learn deeper meaning and anchor the light of the ancient knowledge into their beings. We are grateful for your ongoing focus and attention to the light and the ancient knowledge found within. Vitality, energy, and spirit will be the first focus of attention in this evening's interpretation—this is the way in which the ancient Taoists considered the medicine and is an excellent starting point for the weekend. Integration of spirit, mind, and body are necessary for healing and health. Thought and words are those which create.*

Working with the participants so that they can each embrace their power and responsibility attached with the knowledge of the light will be essential for their ability to embrace and integrate the information of the light and anchor it within their energy centers. Through this energy they may immediately shift their frequency of light into a higher dimension, connecting with specific energy centers in their etheric fields to encourage instantaneous healing for those with whom they come into contact. Many high light beings are ready to interpret this information for the participants.

Encourage your guests to drink plenty of water, cleanse their energy field with lavender, sage, and salt, and to allow themselves plenty of rest to help with assimilation of this information. Some may need dark chocolate high in cacao or some red meat to ground themselves—you have several individuals in attendance who will not utilize these foods as they are against their practice. In this event, offer opportunities for cleansing baths that incorporate apple cider vinegar, baking soda, and sea salt, as well as hot oil treatments so they may be grounded through touch. Salt on the balls of their feet will assist to bring them into their bodies while simultaneously encouraging the anchoring of the light and new information. We are so pleased to have this opportunity to share this information, and we love you very much. We await any questions you may have."

In gratitude, Sarabeth continues the conversation from her own heart. "Thank you so much, dear Metatron. I am so grateful for this information. I have no more questions at this time and am complete. Thank you, all high light beings. Each of you are so dear to me, this information is of great benefit. Thank you all. Archangel Michael, if you could clear the energy, thank you, thank you. Kadosh, kadosh, kadosh. Om mani padme hum. Gate, paragate, parasamgate, Bodhi, svaha!"

Sarabeth opens her eyes. She wipes away the tears that frequently come with the channeling and soothes her throat with another cough drop. She reaches down and pets Leo. As she jots down some notes from the channeling, she is struck by the memory of Lance holding her as he says goodbye; tears streaming down her face.

"I can't imagine my life without you in it," Lance whispers in her ear. Sarabeth feels herself fall into his body as he holds her. Our love is real. I know we are destined to be together, but Rob is so sick now. I feel so torn. And I don't want Sophia to lose the friendship she has with you. I feel lost."

Her reverie is interrupted by a commotion downstairs. Her guests are arriving. She finishes quickly and bounds down the stairs.

Entering through the front door is Laurel Wollenson, whose sparkling green eyes are framed by short blond hair, which makes her look a bit like a pixie.

"Hello, old friend, come in!" Sarabeth says as she hugs Laurel tightly, then motions her into the living room.

"You kept most of your mother's stuff, huh? It really makes the place look great," Laurel says as she looks around at the old adobe walls painted white and the white-washed log ceiling beams running the width of the room. "Such an interesting mix of Santa Fe-style décor with Chinese and French artifacts. Your Mom should have been an interior designer. She would have made a lot of money!"

Sarabeth smiles. "Let's go see your room."

She motions Laurel to follow her down the hall to the last bedroom on the left. "I love this room," she says. "It's so cozy and has great energy!"

Once inside the room, Laurel motions for Sarabeth to shut the door, and then she puts her hands to her lips in a shushing gesture. Sarabeth enters further into the room, close to where Laurel is standing, by the little desk against the window. Laurel opens her jacket and takes out an old newspaper clipping that describes her mother's death almost 35 years ago, when Laurel was just 8 years old. Sarabeth reads it in disbelief. She had never seen it before. The article suggests Laurel's mother may not have died of natural causes, a veiled indication of foul play.

"Laurel, you never told me about this! Why are you showing me now?"

"Sarabeth, one of the people attending this conference has knowledge about how this happened; I am sure of it!"

Sarabeth steps back slightly, stunned. Sitting down in the chair next to the desk she re-reads the newspaper article. Her mind is racing. Her once happy retreat is now the stage for a murder mystery. *I wonder what this is going to bring to bear on this week's events,* she thinks to herself.

Not feeling prepared for the shift in focus and still a bit disconnected because of the channeling, Sarabeth queries Laurel further. "What evidence do you have that one of the participants is the murderer?"

"Well, I've been secretly investigating this murder for five years," Laurel says. "Recently, I uncovered some information that has brought me to this conclusion. I still wrestle in my dreams with what happened that day she died. I was there. I feel I know the person. I just can't seem to put it all together. I almost have everything I need. I can't tell you exactly what I know, but I know the answer is here at this conference. Anyway, I know you have a lot to do to get everyone settled, so let's talk about it later. Sorry for the shock, honey. Oh, and thanks for the room. I really love it."

Laurel turns away, deftly replacing the neatly folded paper into her jacket.

Sarabeth hugs her old friend as she leaves the room.

"You are always full of surprises," she says.

Sarabeth pulls the door shut and stops to breathe. Her heart is racing. She takes a moment to compose her inner center, and then walks back down the hall.

As she passes the kitchen, standing there is her husband, Rob. She stops to give him a hug.

"Well, Laurel is here, and she has quite a story to tell. I'll catch you up later. How's the food from the caterers? Is it what we requested?"

Rob laughs. "Oh yeah, it's great. I can't believe how much food it is. Did you get a chance to channel before you started greeting everyone?"

Sarabeth begins to tell him about the importance of love, and that words and thoughts create meaning and form, when she sees her next two guests walking up the path on the video screen behind Rob on the other side of the kitchen.

"Oh, I have to go meet Jan and Peter. I see them walking up the path now. Love you," she says as she gives Rob a quick kiss on his cheek.

Sarabeth opens the front door just as her friends walk up. They are comfortably dressed and carry themselves as if they are gliding along the ground. They have a gentle, calming disposition. Sarabeth's heart completely relaxes as she sees them.

"Hello, you two, it is so good to see you! Was your travel here uneventful?"

Jan and Peter smile and nod. "It was actually very pleasant and not very long this time," Peter says. "We were in California visiting friends before we came here, so the trip was shorter than usual."

"It's been such a long time since I've seen you," Sarabeth says. "Still, you look even younger than before. What are you doing, eating, or using to create such a youthful transformation? Meditation and herbs, I'm sure!"

Jan and Peter are in their late fifties and yet they look to be in their late thirties: fit but without the sinewy quality that comes with age and over-exercise. They are strong meditators and deeply devoted to each other. They have been working as Ayurvedic and Chinese medicine practitioners for many years and travel often to assist others in their clinical skills or to develop programs for institutions to study the medicine and its positive effects. In their own right they have a strong, detailed, and educated understanding of the work that is the focus of the retreat. They were Sarabeth's teachers in medical school. She is somewhat anxious about their response to the data, but she is so grateful they have come to hear the channeled information.

Jan and Peter warmly hug Sarabeth in a way that seems to assuage any of her fears of offending them and their sensibilities.

"Sarabeth, it is so good to see you—and what an amazing place this is that you have," Jan says as she walks into the foyer. "Peter told me how prestigious it was from when he came to your wedding here 12 years ago. It's more beautiful than I pictured."

Peter pushes back his glasses onto his nose, grabs their two small bags, and walks in behind them wearing a Buddha-smile of true contentment. In that moment, Sarabeth flashes on what Laurel had said—*one of the participants is the murderer.* Sarabeth shakes off the thought like a chill. *These two are the poster images of true peace and contentment. No way they were involved in murder.*

The three of them walk into the living room and sit down on the big, white, embroidered couch. As they relax into the space and look out the picture windows at the beautiful mountains that surround them, there is a slight lull.

"Wow, these are truly amazing artifacts, Sarabeth," Jan says as she holds a cloisonné vase. "It feels so old, and that screen is magnificent! What an interesting life you must have had growing up here."

Sarabeth smiles. "Yes, it was interesting, but more in the way of the Chinese curse, 'May you live in interesting times.' This is not my childhood home, although all of these treasures were present in my early life. So, I wanted to talk with you guys about the first channeling I received just prior to you arriving. In it, the channel revealed information about the early Taoists' beliefs regarding vitality, energy, and spirit. Have you studied that very much, Jan?"

"I did my dissertation on Taoist philosophy," Jan responds.

"The ancient texts are so powerful," Peter says, nodding.

"Yes, my favorite book on the subject is by Thomas Cleary," Jan continues. "He has such a lovely writing voice and clarifies the intention of the work while also connecting the many traditions and showing threads of agreement and evolution. He even suggests and supports the connection of the Greek philosophers like Socrates, Plato, and Aristotle with the Taoists' beliefs about energy and spirit, and how form is known. The most powerful information that I like from his readings of all these philosophers is how thought comes first and then creates form. It is really powerful and connects to the simple tradition that the more substantial follows the least substantial. What you always refer to as qi following shen, and you like to connect it to breath."

Sarabeth laughs out loud.

"Right, Jan! I always used to get that wrong on the tests, replacing 'shen' with 'breath.' I guess to me, breath and shen are interchangeable." Sarabeth smiles. "That is what they talked about today in the message: how thought and words create form."

Jan smiles back. "I'm looking forward to the information and spending time here with you."

"Hey Sarabeth, can we check out our room?" Peter says.

Sarabeth laughs. "Of course! It's right this way. Come on." She walks down the hall to the middle room and turns left.

"This is it. You share the bathroom with my friend Laurel. She is our resident medium. She has a long history of premonitional dreams and 'seeing ghosts.' I think she may have some interesting insights for all of us."

Laurel's words burst into Sarabeth's consciousness. She shrugs her shoulders, trying to move the thoughts out of her mind physically.

Peter touches Sarabeth's back. "Hey, are you OK?"

"Oh, yes, I'm fine. Lots on my mind." Sarabeth smiles sweetly at her friend. "See you later."

Sarabeth hugs both Peter and Jan, then leaves the room quickly. Shutting the door gently, she stops for a moment to reclaim her earlier aplomb. Thinking about Peter, she is reminded that everyone here has extrasensory capacities, so hiding anything is going to be close to impossible. Sooner or later, Laurel's intent is going to come out. Her sweet, connecting gathering is going to have a layer of intrigue and mystery now. Resigning herself to this new wrinkle, she smiles and walks down the hall toward the foyer.

Rob catches up with her in the foyer.

"Hi honey, how is Sophia doing?"

"She is good; she and Laurel are planning... " They both laugh and roll their eyes. "Those two!" Sarabeth shakes her head.

Sophia at 12 is smart beyond her years. She loves nature, and takes walks where she receives information from spirit. Her first book, *Real Fairies in Your Backyard*, was a *New York*

Times bestseller last year. She is now writing a handbook on how to encourage her peers to remain in contact with spirit.

Rob motions to the back room.

"I met up with Bob and Debbie when they came in and showed them to the back room with the separate entrance. Do you think we should have put Peter and Jan in there so they could use the back entrance to go out for their early-morning meditations?"

Sarabeth pauses briefly, and then shakes her head.

"No, this is the best way. Peter and Jan are great at moving around quietly at four in the morning. Debbie and Bob need the space to process information, so the patio off their room will be best for them. I'm going to run down there to say a quick hello, and then let's put out some refreshments. It's already getting late, and we need to do a group channeling today. I'm so excited. Are you?"

Rob, smiling, gives Sarabeth a big hug.

"This is going to be a very powerful time. I can feel it." She gives him a squeeze and walks down the hall.

As she walks away, Rob flashes back to how he almost lost his relationship with Sarabeth and how her loving perseverance, empathic wisdom, and psychic insight saved his life. Suddenly, Lance's face flashes through, and a dark energy rolls over Rob's heart like storm clouds that block the sun in the sky. He shakes it off.

As he watches Sarabeth turn the corner, he jolts out of his reverie. *Shoot, I forgot to clean up my studio*, he thinks. After running up the stairs, he enters his studio, seeing his paints strewn about the two drawing tables facing east toward the mountains. Frantically, he straightens the brushes and paints. Then he turns to the easel and the landscape painting waiting there, reorients it from the door and covers it for now.

Sarabeth knocks gently but clearly on the backroom door. "Debbie? Bob? Are you in there?"

Immediately the door opens. Debbie is hyper and beaming, her thick shoulder-length hair bobbing up and down with each movement and word.

"Sarabeth, so good to see you."

She grabs Sarabeth, hugging her and practically dragging her into the room. "I love this place! Thanks for giving us the big room. It's good for us to have space, especially this backdoor entrance. Perfect! So, are you ready? Are there any little morsels to share? I can't wait for it all to unfold!" Her enthusiasm perks up Sarabeth's mood.

"Yes, Yes! Great information coming through already."

"So? What happened? Where is it all going to go?"

"Well," Sarabeth walks to the loveseat near the window and sits down. "One of the first messages is about how thoughts and words create form; it's simple and yet profound, right?"

"Yes, absolutely." Debbie is moving about the room talking to Sarabeth and unpacking. "I'm ready to go as soon as you are. Just let me know, Sar."

Sarabeth walks over to Debbie, gently touches her on her shoulder to let her know she is going.

"OK, dear, I will see you in a few."

Sarabeth has known Debbie a long enough time that she knows she is now off in her mind, thinking about the consequences of thought and form and whichever philosopher she read recently that said that before—and, of course, how Jung's work fits into the whole thing.

Debbie flings back her thick blonde hair.

"This is just like qi follows shen, you know? Fascinating! See you, Sar."

Sarabeth walks out of the room, firmly closing the door behind her. *Wow*, she thinks to herself, *she is a powerful being, to be sure; I have to remember that I need to sit a bit of a distance away from her while I am channeling. Whew, how does Bob handle it?*

Laurel and Sophia walk out of the opposite room, intensely talking to each other. All are startled.

"Hey there, what's up?" Sarabeth asks.

"Mommy!" Sophia proclaims, as she hugs Sarabeth tightly. "We're going on an adventure. See you later." Laurel looks back at Sarabeth and waves slightly as she is pulled along by Sophia.

"OK, bye honey, have fun you guys." Sarabeth waves as they rush off.

Laurel and Sophia go behind the house, where there's an excavation of dirt in progress.

"See all that dirt? Mom says the last time they did this she found tons of Native American pottery shards, and even a few arrowheads. She was just out of college then, and her Papa said it was an old Native American site long ago. Isn't that cool? Let's find more pottery."

"OK, let's do it," Laurel says with real interest. "Did your mom tell the archeology department at the school?"

"No, I don't think so. Why? Does that make it a crime? Ooh, that would be great, 'cuz my mom never does anything wrong," Sophia says with a smile.

"I don't think so honey. I think it matters if it's someone else's property but not your own, and it would have been your Papa's responsibility, so your mom is probably off the hook."

"Oh, OK."

Immediately they begin finding shards of red and black pottery. Both are very excited as they gather it up.

CHAPTER 2

The human body is only vitality, energy, and spirit. Vitality, energy, and spirit are called the three treasures. Ultimate sagehood and noncontrivance are both attained from these. Few people know these three treasures, even by way of their temporal manifestations. What is inconceivable is their primordial state—is it not lost? If you lose these three treasures, you are incapable of noncontrivance, and so are unaware of the primordial.

—Lu Yan, the ancestor of the Complete Reality School of Taoism.

Taoism perceives that the originators of civilization itself are people of higher knowledge attained through extradimensional awareness...all successful original cultures are initiated and guided by people in contact with the Tao or universal law.

—Thomas Cleary

To discover the Tao, enter and observe nature.

—The I Ching

All in the universe is intricately connected as one, one breath, one body. It is observable through the unified field theory of Albert Einstein.

—Mike Cohen

Excitedly entering the backyard, Laurel and Sophia are covered in dirt; pieces of pottery are overflowing in their arms. Sophia is holding several obsidian arrowheads the way she once held her ice skating medals.

Rob yells out from the kitchen.

"Hi you guys! We're meeting in the living room for the first channeling in about 20 minutes. Hurry up."

Sophia runs up to him.

"Dad, look what we found, isn't it so cool?"

"Wow, that is a lot! Nice specimens too. I bet you're excited."

"I am" Sophia proclaims, and then runs upstairs to her room.

"Remember to wash up," Rob calls out after her. "I hope she heard me," he says to Laurel. "You too."

"OK," Laurel says. She takes the treasures to her room.

Sarabeth lights some incense and rings her toning bowls to clear the room before the channeling. The chairs are placed slightly away from her so she can be surrounded by her own energy. Finding a comfortable position on her white, embroidered couch, she closes her eyes and begins to seal the space around her as she prepares to go within.

In the hall, Debbie and Bob greet Peter and Jan.

"Hi, I'm Dr. Debbie Hanolin, and this is my husband, Dr. Bob Yangxue."

Jan greets Debbie and Bob.

"Hello, we're Drs. Jan Talent and Peter Venaglia," she says quietly.

"So, how did you find out about this workshop?" Debbie asks. "Did you guys have a connection to Sarabeth?"

"We were her professors when she was studying in China," Peter responds. "She had this natural understanding of how to balance the pulses and bring her patients into harmony. She seemed to intuitively connect the pulses with spirit as if she received information directly from source, like she was channeling information about underlying issues with patients. Her point protocols were these innovative, divine ways to extinguish disease. It was pretty awesome to watch. What about you guys? How did you meet Sarabeth?"

"Interestingly, in a very similar way. We met when we moved here to practice," Debbie answers. "We are traditionally trained as Jungian analysts, but we each have Chinese heritage: Bob was born in Hong Kong and educated in London, and we met on the East Coast. I was trained in Santa Fe. Bob met Sarabeth while he was filming a documentary on empathic healing. I met Sarabeth through clients we shared in common. It's been a powerful collaboration to work together. It is as if she receives information through some extraordinary form of observation and listening."

"We've stayed in touch over the years as we have each evolved our practices," Peter says. "Our work includes other training as well, and we each integrate several different traditional medicines in our treatment strategies."

"I'm excited to get a view into the way she receives the information," Debbie comments. "I haven't experienced the channeling before. I'm hoping the information that comes through will uplevel my skills and offer some new ways to help my clients."

"So did your family have information about oriental medicine in your heritage?" Peter asks Bob.

"Not exactly. We had techniques and herbs we would use under specific conditions to treat illness, but it wasn't called oriental medicine. It was like a home remedy. It included cupping for colds and stagnation-type diseases, blood-moving herbs, and calming herbs. We even used a tool like a guasha tool for muscle injuries, but I had to learn about the medicine through my studies. Only the actions and procedures were passed down, not the why-for's. Debbie had some too, but her heritage is farther back, so it was even more disjointed."

"Very nice," Peter says. "Let's go in."

The four walk into the living room. Laurel and Rob are sitting in chairs near Sarabeth.

Sarabeth greets everyone.

"Hello! I am so glad we are all here."

Sophia walks in just then and takes a seat near her mom. Sarabeth switches off the music from her phone and silence envelops the room.

The sound of cars driving by offers a soothing, humming, rhythmic energy. The peaceful sound lulls everyone into quiet, inward focus.

Beginning her normal procedure for channeling, Sarabeth starts speaking in a gentle, lilting voice.

"Welcome. Please, everyone sit in a comfortable position and invite in your healing guides. I know some of you have been to a channeling before, so you know the process. However, I'm going to speak it out loud so that we can jointly focus inward and prepare ourselves for the immense energy. I apprenticed with two amazing spiritual women, Leigh and Morgan, who both cleared negative energy through various physical processes—mainly burping, coughing, and sneezing—so, I do too! Please, excuse me in advance."

Sarabeth smiles at everyone. She burns some sage, clearing the energy for the channeling to commence.

"Oh, and they also seemed to use a yawning method to uplevel consciousness as the energy got higher, so if you feel the need to do this yourself, it's natural. You may feel a surge of energy, dizziness, or a swirling sense within you, a deep sense of calm, or feel tears—all cues that spirit is entering, and you are moving into a higher dimension of consciousness. I have placed bowls of dark chocolate bars, peanut clusters, and peanut butter energy bars, as well as lozenges. You each have water nearby too. These items help assimilate the high energy that comes through, and they assist in grounding you once the channeling is complete."

Sarabeth puts a lozenge into her mouth and takes several deep, cleansing breaths as she begins her opening mantra. "OK, let's begin."

"*Dear god, goddess, and great spirit, allow me to be a clear healing channel. I call in a hundred thousand angels to please come in and fill this room; I invite in only high-frequency light beings. Please come in to guide me and offer me interpretation for this first evening of this retreat on healing psycho-emotional trauma through the ancient traditions...Thank you for your protection and guidance dear Archangel Michael, Metatron, Orion, Sirius, the Council of Twelve, and the Marys...* "

Sarabeth feels the voice and words from the channel and begins to simply speak what is presented to her. Her voice lightens and deepens, gaining increased softness as she speaks the words as if they are her own, instantly knowing the content as she herself hears the words from her own voice:

"*Dearly beloved, we are here and we want you to know how much we love you and your friends assembled here today. We are grateful for your work in upleveling the light on the planet. You all have been shining stars in your various fields to help the planet anchor the light. This is about bringing increased light into your vessels as you choose to have this experience; several of you have already made an intention to open further to your healing traditions. All is energy and light.*

"*Love is the best emotion on which to focus your attention and is the most healing response. Acceptance, allowing, and love. Through love you will open the door to access deeper meaning and anchor the light of the ancient knowledge into your beings. Love is the way, as it expands your heart. It is through your heart center that you anchor the light into your being. An open and boundaried heart center has the capacity to anchor a higher frequency of light and allows you as a vessel to vibrate at a higher healing frequency.*

"*We are grateful for your ongoing focus and attention to the light and the ancient knowledge found within. Vitality, energy, and spirit are the first focus of attention in this evening's interpretation. This is the way in which the ancient Taoists considered the medicine and is an excellent starting point for the weekend. Integration of spirit, mind, and body are necessary for healing and health.*

"Thought and words are those which create. All is created out of thought and words: Attention and intention, focus, energy, and creation...you create that to which you put your attention. Emotions and feelings are the key. Pay attention to that which brings you joy, that which you desire, and this is what you will create. Be open without and centered within. The energy works thusly: Pay attention to that which you fear, or to that which is lacking, and you create more of that fear and lacking; flip back and forth between the two attentions and you create a stagnation or spiral between fear and joy fulfillment and lack. You choose your creation through your attention and intention, and love. Your heart center is your guiding force. Pay attention to what brings you joy, gratitude, and care, and you create more of that. Your way is the way of the heart. Love, compassion, and gratitude are the foci through which you create healing and prosperity.

"Embrace your power and honor your responsibility to the knowledge of the light. This is essential; for your ability to integrate and embrace the information of the light and anchor it within your energy centers. This can be destabilizing at first. Be gentle and loving toward yourself as you integrate the light into your being. To the degree you can anchor the light into your being you will shift your energy into a higher dimension. You may connect with those energy centers in your etheric field, within your body, and aligning you from above, at 6 inches, 12 inches, 18 inches, several feet, and 12 feet above your crown chakra. Your capacity to heal is directly related to the amount of light you are able to anchor through your system, and so, as you develop this, with loving-kindness toward yourself, you develop the opportunity for others to instantly heal in your presence, if it is in their highest good and part of their integrated soul plan. Remember that you may not change another's plan without their permission.

"In order to anchor the light, you may need to practice stretching of your spine through yoga. Additionally, for your full understanding of the unified field theory, create daily, silent time with nature so

you can practice hearing and connecting with the subtle energy of communication with all of nature.

"Vitality, energy, and spirit align you with the nature of things. These are the three bases. Vitality is the root of essence and life within the body. In the heavens it is the sun and moon and stars, the milky way; energy is the activity, awareness, perception, speech and thoughts—the intention and attention within the body. Spirit is the true director, the light, the recognition of senses, the instinct within the body—in the heavens it is the true director, compassion, dignity, the force of creation, the basis of the origin of all beings.

"Several of us have spoken in this time: Ancestor Lu, Sirius, the Marys, Archangel Metatron, and the Council of Twelve. Many high light beings are ready to channel loving guidance and information for the participants. We are available for specific questions...remember to drink plenty of water to help you at the cellular level as you are integrating this information and increasing the degree and frequency of light you are each holding. Cleanse your energy field with lavender and sage, as well as salt and baking soda. Allow yourselves plenty of rest to help with assimilation of this information. Some of you may need dark chocolate or some red meat to ground yourselves; we know there are three of you who will not utilize these foods as they are against your practice. You may use cleansing baths that incorporate apple cider vinegar and sea salt, as well as hot oil treatments so you may be grounded through touch. Salt on the balls of your feet will assist to bring you into your bodies while simultaneously encouraging the anchoring of the light and new information.

"We are so pleased to have this opportunity to share this information. We love you very much...we await any questions you may have."

"Thank you so much Sirius, the Marys, The Council of Twelve, Ancestor Lu, and Archangel Metatron. I am so grateful for this information. At this time, I will open it up to questions...please begin from my left."

Sarabeth motions to her left as Jan speaks first.

"Hello and thank you for coming through for us. Could you talk more about the Taoists' concept of vitality, energy, and spirit? How is this useful in assisting individuals in clearing disease?"

"Hello Jan, first we want you to know we are intimately aware of your work on the planet and are so very grateful for the love you bring to your students and colleagues. Vitality, energy, and spirit are your ways in, your entrance points, for the integration of the vessel with whom you are working. Focus on the vitality, the physical being, the energetic field of the vessel and their connection to source. All are of the utmost importance, as you are knowledgeable about how energy flows from least to most substantial. You are aware that spiritual disconnects, blocked emotions, and unclear thinking can lead to masses and disruptions in the physical vessel. The ideas set forth by the Taoists regarding vitality, energy, and spirit are very useful for you to reexamine in order to focus how you work with others.

"Collecting body and mind is gathering medicine. She who understands the relationship of three, five, and one, she is a practitioner who collects body and mind, and allows for unification of the three, allowing for flow and balance. The three bases: vitality, energy, and spirit lead to the five forces: essence, sense, spirit, vitality, and will, and finally lead to the five elements: wood, metal, fire, water, and earth. To understand and recognize the elements in human beings, follow the ancient Taoists. Watch the way the elements move and behave in nature. As you do this, the invisible Tao becomes visible through its reflection in the natural world.

"If you all will begin to work at the energetic fields, you can encourage your contacts to develop their internal connection to spirit and their internal guidance system. Use the directions and how these gather to assist in healing. East three is essence, and connects with wood; south two is spirit, and connects with fire; these together relate to the mind; north one is vitality and connects with water; west four is sense and connects with metal; these together relate to the body; the center five is will and connects with earth. It focuses the integration of all and action. This is the way to collect body and mind and to practice

gathering medicine. This is the way through love and light, to increase integration of spirit, mind, and body toward each being's highest and best action and creation. You may do this in an integrated fashion, addressing all three centers: shen, spirit; qi, energy; and xue, blood or the corporeal body. You will find that western science is focusing on the essence of Jing through increased understanding of the HLA patternings and the double helix DNA strands. This can be a lovely way to incorporate integrated movement with the traditional and western medicines. Studying in this direction while translating this new science through the historical Taoist teaching of the three treasures will increase your success in this area. Does this answer your question?"

"Yes, this is excellent. Can I use toning to help to integrate the three, five, and one to access the three bases, the five elements or forces, and the centering of energetic will?"

"Yes, dear one, we smile and hold you up, for you understand this clever medicine and have a beautiful, delicate style of standing on the planet at this time. Your kundalini energy has risen high into your crown chakra, and you are capable of sage-hood with non-contrivance and developing a sweet awareness of the primordial Tao. More will be revealed in a future translation; however, you can ponder not only the use of toning bowls but also the sounding of the of the vowel sounds in your own body or with your clients. Pronounce the vowels in this way to align spirit, mind, and body: e = Aa, i = ee, a = ah, o = o, u = oo. This allows for you and the client to see where blockages or physical, emotional, or spiritual traumas may have diverted the natural order of the qi meridians, causing a disconnect from the client's soul path and a disease process in the body. As the client focuses her intention and attention into the sound as it resonates through her, she will be able to release old patternings and trauma. Continue your work, dear one."

"Oh gracious, sage-hood is too much, I daresay—I am only a student of the Tao. I will ponder this further in my meditation and continue to focus on love and light." Jan then sits back, lost in her thoughts.

"May I ask one more question?" Rob says.

"Yes. *Sarabeth is beginning to tire, so one more question will be all for today.*"

"OK. Sarabeth, are you OK?"

"Yes, honey, I have enough energy to go on."

"OK, I'm wondering about the process of using emotions as an internal sensory guidance structure to stay in the light, and wonder if anger is an effective or ineffective emotion for guidance. I struggle with this, and when I have researched this in reading, it seems there is some dissonance from the ancient traditions about the usefulness of fear and anger."

"Rob, this is a wonderful question to elucidate what is powerful and guiding about emotions. Each of you are experiencing life multi-dimensionally. Dissonance can appear when there is a lack of cognitive or intentional connection to your soul purpose or a mental pushing against the flow of the natural order. Anger offers an opportunity for you to discover where you are not taking responsibility for your creation, or where there is a lack of congruence in action by a group-think or community action. Fear and anger are also present when you are being driven by a personality or the secondary drive rather than soul purpose-driven behavior. Observe anger as a guide to see where a boundary has been crossed—emotional, physical, or spiritual. This can lead to increased connection, increased communication, and an internal realignment in word, thought, and deed with your highest purpose. Look for the source of your anger and lightly drop below the emotion to your true soul purpose. Because fear and anger are emotions connected to a sense of physical safety, it is sometimes difficult to extricate yourself from the intensity and experience of it. Your perspective of the situation may need to be changed. Recognize that all relationships are a reflection of your inner process, so that you can shift your perspective from victim to creator. When anger comes up, look within for a historical trigger or patterning that is being repeated. At a deeper level, look for how you may be disconnected from the high light frequencies. This can allow for a shift in perspective and increased understanding of the situation. Awareness is insufficient for

change; action is also required to shift your circumstance, eradicate the patterning, and evolve into a more integrated creator. The high light frequencies assist you in elevating your consciousness into a more integrated path directed by your soul and the experiencing of divine love. Loving-kindness, self-compassion, and recognition of your full power in everything that you create will assist you in shifting how you experience the emotion of anger and fear. Through these qualities you can use your knowledge and cognitive skills driven by the concept of heart centered action to guide your actions toward a more neutral response and aligned approach. Does this answer your question?"

"Yes, this gives me information with which I can further investigate. Thank you."

Sarabeth gently wipes tears from her eyes. "Thank you, all high light beings, for your support and your information today. Each of you is of great benefit. Thank you all. Archangel Michael, if you could clear the energy, thank you, thank you. Kadosh, kadosh, kadosh. Om mani padme hum. Gate, gate, paragate, parasamgate, Bodhi, svaha."

As Sarabeth opens her eyes, she is surprised by the sheer hush in the room. It is as if her friends are all in a trance.

"Well, you guys, what do you think? It was a beautiful and very full message, right?"

Sophia goes over and gives her a hug.

"Mom, it was really extraordinary and very long. Are you OK?"

"Oh yes, but I'm a little ungrounded. I think we should eat and get back into our bodies. That was a very high frequency of light. Rob and I have some wonderful grounding food from our favorite vegetarian Ayurvedic place in town. So, Jan and Peter, you are going to be happy and well cared for."

Sarabeth smiles.

"Laurel, you may want to eat that food too. And I'm sure you will join them, right Sophia?"

"Yes, it's my favorite! I want samosas, and kitchari!"

Debbie quietly speaks up.

"Wow, Sarabeth, I had no idea. This is really going to be interesting. Can we also ask personal, specific questions while you are channeling? Can you channel answers to these?"

"Oh yes, absolutely. The bulk of the information that is being offered comes in first from the beings who show up, but once the entity completes that and offers a time for questioning, you are free to ask whatever is of interest to you. It is really astounding what you can discover. I think Laurel has something she is interested in inquiring about, too."

Laurel looks a bit uneasy at this remark from Sarabeth and shifts in her seat.

"Well, I don't know...maybe, we'll see."

She looks over at Sarabeth with a note of irritation that she has referenced her secret.

Sarabeth smiles at Laurel sweetly, and then looks back to the whole group.

"Oh, and there are some meat offerings for dinner, too. Are you ready? You seem a bit stuck there in those seats. Move your bodies around a bit, and you can slap the ball of your foot at about kidney 1 on the acupuncture meridians if you need more assistance in getting into your bodies."

Peter immediately slaps his left foot.

"Oh, that is better, how interesting."

Rob does too, and Debbie.

"That's just weird," she says.

"Yes, we were pretty far up there. Some of you may want to go to sleep early tonight; and please, feel free to take baths or do the hot oil treatments. Or you can even do some warm oil massage in the shower if you prefer. Let's go eat!"

The group follows Sarabeth into the kitchen through the door at the other end of the living room. All the food is set up on the counter facing them, buffet style, with little cards in Sophia's handwriting describing each dish.

Laurel shifts away from the group, leaving the living room by the door near the front door and hallway. Passing the kitchen from the other side, she moves undiscovered. She goes back to her room and gets out her file on her mother's death. There are articles, pictures, and lots of hand-written notes she has collected over the last five years about her mother's death. She pulls out a well-worn notebook and looks at the information inside. She is searching for a name. She finds it: Debbie H. She looks for the article and notes relating to her. She retrieves a corkboard from her closet that she brought with her to the retreat. It has bits of paper pinned to it with connections from the articles to her mom and incidents leading to and after her death. She pins the article and notes about Debbie H. onto the corkboard with her name. Then she sits down, staring at the board, trying to solve the equation.

She is sparked out of her daydream by a knock on her door. It's Sarabeth in the hallway.

"Honey, are you in there? Don't be mad at me for focusing on you. No one knows what you're up to. Honey, are you in there?"

Laurel sees that Sarabeth is turning the doorknob.

"Yes, yes, I'm here, just a minute."

The doorknob stops turning. Laurel quickly puts away the corkboard.

"Here I am, Beth," Laurel says as she opens the door.

"Oh, OK honey. You only call me Beth when you are feeling sweetly toward me, so I guess you aren't that mad." Sarabeth smiles. "Let's go get some food, Elle."

She hugs her friend, and they walk down the hallway toward the kitchen.

Laurel thinks about how she can get into Debbie's room to do some investigative work as they enter the kitchen.

CHAPTER 3

"*The general function of dreams is to try to restore our psychological balance by producing dream material that re-establishes, in a subtle way, the total psychic equilibrium.*"

—Carl Jung, Psychology of the Unconscious

"*Where love rules, there is no will to power, and where power predominates, love is lacking. The one is the shadow of the other.*"

—Carl Jung, Man and his Symbols

Jan and Peter quietly shut the door to their room. It's early morning. Jan hears a commotion at the end of the hall: muffled crying. She looks at Peter as if to say, should we go down and check? He shakes his head and motions for the front door.

Carrying their mats, they walk quietly down the hall moving toward the front patio for their morning meditation and yoga practice. A light in the kitchen helps them to not lose their way—a kind gift from Sarabeth, who knows they leave to meditate while it's still dark. Jan smiles to herself. As they get to the door Peter stops, all of a sudden worried about an alarm on the door. Jan bumps into him and looks up, a bit frustrated, with a look of confusion. Peter points to the alarm next to the door, which is blinking red. Jan pats him on the shoulder and points to a note taped to the door: "Don't worry, the alarm is disabled. Enjoy your meditation. Love, Sarabeth" it says. Peter has to cover his mouth to not laugh out loud. Giggling quietly, they both walk to the front patio.

Down the hall, more muffled crying.

A very small child is walking down the hall of her home to her mother and dad's room. Sitting on the bed is her father. She looks at him; he is distraught, holding a pill box in his hand, shaking his head, saying over and over, "How did this happen? How did this happen?" The little girl looks over to her mother, limp on the bed with a sweet, calm smile on her face.

The child goes to her mother and touches her arm. "Mommy, are you... ? She pauses. Her mother's arm is ice cold. "Mommy?"

"Daddy, what's wrong with Mommy?"

"She's gone, honey."

"No, Daddy, no! How could this happen? I need her to stay with me."

"I know honey, I want her with us too; I know how hard this is for you. Don't worry, you aren't alone, I will be there for you twice as much now that you don't have Mom, and we will keep her memory alive with love. Come here, honey, let me hold you."

"Daddy, it's not fair, it's not fair. I want my mommy."

The little girl crumbles in her father's arms, crying in big heaves... then little sobs. She falls asleep with her father holding her.

Suddenly, Laurel awakens. Her pillow is soaked with tears, the smell of her mother still in her memory. She turns over to look at a picture of her mother, father, and herself, the little girl in the dream. She says to the picture, "I still miss you, Mom." She looks over at the clock: 4 a.m.

"Great, now what am I supposed to do?" she mumbles to herself.

She gets out of bed and goes over to the corkboard. She stares at the connections, trying to solve the equation of how her mother died. The medicine bottle is the key. But since her dad died five years ago, she can't deliberate with him about what he meant.

I have to figure out how to ask the channel the question so as to not tip off the person I'm after, she thinks to herself. Sarabeth says the answer you really seek is what the channel gives you, so I have to be careful.

She stares at the corkboard, trying to remember the name on the medicine bottle.

Across the hall, Debbie and Bob are sweetly talking about the information from the day before. They both have studied Chinese medicine and Taoist theory in relation to Jungian theory for many years.

"Somehow, this is related to the five phases and the ghost treatments, but how? What do you think, Bob?"

"It definitely has the energy of the collective unconscious in the way in which the cycle can be affected by energy stagnation and release. Debbie, did you bring any of our books with us?"

"Yes, of course, several. I think she has WiFi here too, so we can get online and do a search. This is so exciting to be able to have a way into that ancient knowledge, not translated but interpreted from a higher source. It is so cool. I cannot wait until tonight. We get a channeling each evening, right?"

"Yes. What do you want to do today before the channeling? I was thinking it would be nice to talk with Peter; he seems so well versed in Chinese medicine. Sarabeth said Peter trained with a master in China who held information about the medicine before it was cleansed of references to spirit. What an interesting history. I really want to talk to him."

"Yes, I agree, he and Jan are really interesting. It's very exciting to have the opportunity to get to know them. We could perhaps take a walk with them or just meet them for lunch. But for sure, I want to get into some of the ancient texts to see how similar the information is to what is written there. This channeling stuff is exciting! I'm interested in talking with Laurel, too. Sarabeth said Laurel is able to see and talk with ghosts, and I thought I might find out about what happened with my family back in China. Although I guess I could also ask the channel. As soon as I heard she had these talents I immediately thought of asking her about an old friend. It's so early, I think I'm going to get some coffee, and then sit out here on our side patio. How sweet of Sar to make sure we had this space to relax and discuss our thoughts together. Do you want me to get you some coffee? I am pretty sure she will have a latte machine."

"Yes, that sounds great," Bob said, absentmindedly. He has picked up one of the books and is reading it while Debbie talks. Debbie shuts the door behind her; smiling, she walks down the hall to the kitchen.

"Mom, I had the most amazing dream. Will you listen to me for a minute?" Sophia exasperatedly sighs.

"OK, tell me what happened."

"Well, it was a long time ago because people were wearing these really beautiful coats and outfits, like what we wear when we celebrate Chinese New Year. It was really cool. Hi Debbie, I think you'll like this dream too, since you're kind of Chinese, and we always celebrate Chinese New Year with you. Sit down with us."

Debbie smiles at Sarabeth. "Good morning, dear," she says. They hug sweetly.

Then, nodding toward Sophia, she says, "Can I make a latte while I listen to your dream?"

Yes, I guess so, but it's kind of loud. OK, anyway, the dream was a little fuzzy, like in shadow. It was nighttime. I know because the moon was shining through a window of this really cool house made of stone, kind of like a castle. There was this man sitting at a table. He was writing in a book, but it's an old style, like we saw in the movie *The Sorcerer's Apprentice*. You know, where the ink was in a small pot and he was using a brush. The writing was Chinese—beautiful characters. He was writing, and he was working very seriously. It was really cool. The writing was a really bright part of the dream, very clear, and I could see the characters on the page that he was making. In the dream I knew what the characters meant, but I can't remember right now.

"So, there was all this focus on the writing, and I'm a little girl watching the writing from another room in the palace. I know I'm not supposed to be there, but I'm watching, hidden in the doorway shadow. Then—this is the scary part—someone comes in and hits the person on the head and knocks him out. I pull back further into the shadow, and then he does something with the writing: He takes it all. All the books the first man had written, and he puts them in a satchel, and then he just leaves. I go into the room to check on the man but he doesn't move. He is very still. I think he's dead! And then I woke up. What do you think about that? Oh, and there was one more thing: The man's name, it was written in Chinese characters on a book on the desk. Of course, I don't know what it was, but I think I can remember the characters. Hey Debbie, do you think you could decipher his name?"

"Maybe, it kind of depends. You know, Chinese has different ways of writing in different time periods. Why don't you write them down and I will try. I'll show them to Bob, too. He is better with the language."

"OK cool, thanks! I'm going to Dad's studio to work on it. Bye Mom, I love you. Bye Debbie." Sophia runs up the stairs above the living room to Rob's study, two at a time.

"So, Sarabeth, have you taught her how to look at her dreams for messages?"

"Yes, a bit, but she has dreams that contain remnants of past lives as well as dreams of possible futures, so I mostly just listen. Sometimes, if I'm nervous, I will query about some particulars. I am sure that's why she identified which parts of the dream were strongest and clearest. She may have incorporated my questions into her process of how she tells me the dreams. I know you picked up on the writing being the most important part."

"It is interesting that she understood the language while in the dream, and it feels past-life-*ish*, not that that is a word."

"Yeah, I know. Well, let's see what we get when she finishes the drawing of the characters. After that, we can determine if we should be doing more investigative work on the dream. I know with your background you really perk up when it comes to a dream."

"I love the channeling. It is incredible! What is it like for you, as the channel? Do you remember what is said? And how do you keep your own ideas or cognitions out of the whole thing, especially when the channel is saying stuff you actually have information about or training in? That has to be so hard."

"It takes practice to not get my stuff in the way. It's a lot like yoga, actually; well, that's how I describe it. The harder I try, the less I get. The more I relax and allow, the more I get. You know how in yoga, when you're trying a new position and you really try to put yourself into the position, you can pull a muscle or you kind of work against yourself? But if you relax into the position, with breath and a light, open intention and allowing, you can get even further into the position than you had imagined. It's exactly the same with channeling. It's a flow. So, just like with all flow, I can't push it. It all comes from my heart-space rather than my mind. My *heart-openness* is the leader, and my mind follows. There are things I have to think about and set up beforehand so that I am protected and open to only high light beings; and there are things I need to think about when I complete the channeling and go through the cleansing for myself and the participants and room. But the middle part—the core of it, the channeling—that is all heart. It's really a beautiful, intimate experience, pure love-energy. I almost always well up with tears, and when I am clearing someone, the depth of feeling can be really sensory, painful, and intense."

"Amazing. I'm really looking forward to tonight. OK, I'm off. I want to catch up with Jan. She seems so knowledgeable and interesting. I cannot wait to talk with her about the medicine and her take on how it relates to Jung."

"OK, good luck, and have fun. You may get further with Jan if you talk with her about Jung via five-phase theory. You know the five elements—that's going to be your common language. Oh, don't you want to bring this latte to Bob?"

"Oh yes, thanks; and thanks for the tip. It's amazing to watch Sophia. She is really something."

Sarabeth smiles at Debbie as she watches her walk back down the hallway. Drinking her latte, she reminisces about Sophia and her early psychic ability; especially how often she knew what Sarabeth or Rob were thinking. *It was a little scary in the beginning*, she thinks to herself, as small flashes reappear of incidents when Sophia was telepathic. *Sitting at the stoplight, thinking about cutting her hair and hearing this small voice emanating from 3-year-old Sophia in her car seat: 'No, Mommy, I don't want you to cut your hair!' Sophia playing with money she found in Sarabeth's wallet. 'How much money do you have there?' Sophia looking at Rob and Sarabeth and exclaiming, 'It's 60.' Rob and I locking eyes and asking her, 'How did you know that?' And Sophia saying, 'I can hear you talking in your minds.' I'm lucky my own inner-sight or see-knowings helped me normalize it for Rob and Sophia. It was difficult at first, but over time it seemed to fade into more of a sensitivity to information rather than a direct download of our minds, which made privacy easier between Rob and me. I wonder how they will continue to develop with age.*

Rob walks into the kitchen.

"Hi honey, what's up? Do you want to do some yoga with me before we start our day?"

Sarabeth warmly smiles at Rob.

"Yes, absolutely. Let's go into the den. Or do you want to go on the back patio?"

"Let's go into the den. I already have it set up in there."

"Hi you guys. We just finished," Peter and Jan call into the den as they pass. "But can we join you two for a second set?"

"Yes, of course, come on in. How was your meditation this morning?"

"I felt reinvigorated by the channeling from last night, so it was great for me," Jan says as she sets up her mat.

"What about you, Peter? How was your meditation?"

"Really good. I actually had a few insights about some of the information. It's really exciting. After this I'm going to go check out a new theory with one of the Chinese Medicine books we brought with us just for reference. It's a really old manuscript I received early in my training."

Laurel is finally feeling a little better after her difficult awakening and dream. She sees the group in the den doing yoga and goes into the kitchen for some coffee. Bob is sitting at the counter with his latte, rereading one of his favorite books, when he sees her.

"Hey, Laurel. What's up?"

"Not much. I feel a little out of sorts this morning. What are you up to?"

"I'm waiting for Peter. I want to talk with him about some of the information we heard last night. He is such an expert on this stuff. I'm interested in his take on it all."

"Huh, cool. What's Debbie doing?"

Laurel thinks she could investigate their room for clues if they were both going to be gone—not that she knows exactly what she is looking to find.

"Uh, Debbie is going to catch up with Jan. I think she has some questions for her. Do you want to join them? I know that Debbie wanted to see if she could ask you something about a death that has been bothering her for years. Sarabeth told her that you talk to dead people. Is that true?"

"Oh, she told her that, huh? Well yes, it is true, but I only have marginal control over who comes in, so sometimes it isn't that helpful."

Laurel thinks how frustrating it is that she cannot connect with her mother to solve her mystery.

"I would be happy to try for Debbie, though. Just let me know."

"Great."

Bob returns to his book as Laurel, lost in her thoughts, continues to make her latte.

Debbie enters and almost pounces on Laurel.

"Hi Laurel."

"Hi Debbie. You seem very happy and energetic."

"Yeah, I'm always this way, sorry. Listen, I was wondering if I could talk to you about something?"

"Don't say I didn't warn you," Bob says to Laurel.

Smiling at Bob, Laurel says, "Sure, but you should know that I can't always contact the person you want. There are all sorts of reasons why, but suffice it to say, I just open, and whomever can come through does. So, it may not be very satisfying."

"How did you... " Debbie looks confused at Laurel, then says, "Oh, Bob told you; OK, no problem. When can we do this?"

"We can do it later today. Maybe early afternoon, before the channeling. I'm not in a very good space right now."

"Oh, OK. Are you all right? I don't want to pressure you."

"Oh, it's nothing to worry about. I'll be better in a few hours, I'm sure."

"OK, great, talk to you then."

Debbie then turns to Bob.

"Honey, I'm going to try to grab Jan; I think they are almost finished."

Debbie hugs Bob as she leaves the kitchen.

"OK, dear, see you later."

"She's been bothered by this person's death half of her life, so thanks for helping her, Laurel."

Laurel smiles at Bob as she walks out of the room onto the back patio.

"No problem."

The sun in the backyard is so strong and clear, it really helps Laurel's mood. Sarabeth steps outside and warmly greets Laurel.

"Hey there, how are you doing?"

"I'm doing a lot better now. I had this terrible dream. This dream always throws me off. It's about the day my mom died. Something keeps bothering me about it. The dream keeps coming back. I am sure my subconscious is trying to show me something important, but I'm not able to see the message—it's so frustrating. And every time I wake up from the dream the pain is like when I was a kid. It really skews my energy."

"Oh, I'm sorry, Laurel. Do you want me to give you a treatment to clear the energy?"

"No, the sun is really helping, actually."

"OK. Let me know if you want to talk."

"I will."

The two women sit quietly enjoying the sun. After a while, Sarabeth gets up to go inside.

"See you later, Laurel."

Upstairs in the studio, Rob and Sophia are working on the Chinese characters.

"Dad, it isn't exactly like that. Let me show you."

Sophia takes the calligraphy brush and reworks the strokes.

"It's more like this. See how curvy it is?"

"Oh, I see, OK. Do you want me to do that kind of stroke for all the characters?"

"Yes, I think that's it."

Rob goes through his books to find one on Chinese characters.

"I think we have a book that can help us with deciphering the meaning of the characters and maybe the person's name."

"Dad, do you think that I actually had a dream about a real thing—like, a real thing that happened?"

"I don't know, honey. Those kinds of dreams aren't very common. But you do have strong intuitive skills and talents at connecting with spirit, so, maybe."

"I think it's really sad if it happened, because that unknown assailant—you know, the guy who hit the scholar, well, he stole all of his work. That makes me really sad."

Sophia starts to cry.

Rob stops his work and steps over to Sophia.

"It's OK, honey. I understand how you're feeling. I think it's great that you are sensitive."

He continues to hug Sophia. "You better now?"

Sophia brightens.

"Yes."

"OK, so let's see if you can remember anything else from the dream that can help us identify the time period, and the person, in time. Do you remember what the books were about? What was he writing about?"

"Well, I was thinking about that, and I thought maybe it was about the stuff that Mom channeled about because, well, why else would I have had the dream last night, right?"

"Oh, that is an interesting point. Good critical thinking, honey. OK, so Mom was channeling about the Taoist period, right? I remember her saying something about the Taoists.

What do you remember? Since it was your dream, it has something to do with your thoughts about what Mom said."

"Right, OK, so what I started to think about was the Yellow Emperor, but was he Taoist? I also was thinking about that movie *The Sorcerer's Apprentice* and Merlin, 'cuz it was all about transformation and light. What time period was that supposed to be?"

"Hmm, you know, I don't know. This is not my specialty. We should get Mom to help us."

Sarabeth enters the studio after leaving Laurel on the back patio.

"Help you with what?"

"Mom! Hi! We are working on the letters, and Dad thinks it may be about a real thing—like, a real event. So, we're doing some investigative work, but we need your help with history. Will you help us?"

"Sure honey, what do you need?"

Sarabeth stands over the letters and looks at the book.

"Hmm, so I heard you say something about the Yellow Emperor, and the Taoists. What are you trying to do?"

"We're trying to connect the dream in time."

"Oh, that's an interesting idea. You know, one of the beings that channels through me says that time is really not as linear as we think and that we may be living in multi-dimensions, so I wonder if what you dreamed was a possible thread in time. Of course, that will make it way harder to decipher, so maybe we should work from a linear perspective to begin our task."

Rob looks at Sarabeth with one of his *Really? That's where you're going with this?* looks and says, "Yeah, let's do that."

Sarabeth smiles wryly at him.

"OK, so the basic ideas of the *Huangdi Neijing* are attributed to the Yellow Emperor. It's probably many authors compiled under this one mythic character. It is Taoist in nature. The work that the light being was interpreting to us yesterday was more in line with what was written by Hua To and Ancestor Lu, also called Lu-Yen, and other important Taoist writers."

Sarabeth continues to think out loud as she looks at the books in front of her.

"The most well-known Taoist treatise is the *Tao Te Ching*, which we quote all the time when considering how to get back to center and balance. It is attributed to Lao Tzu, but you may not know that most scholars state that it is unlikely that a single individual developed this composition. So anyway, a lot of what was being referenced is from these writings more than the *Neijing*, I think. All of these writers are in generally the same time period—but that includes hundreds of years. So, how to pinpoint this image in time, and to which writings the dream is attempting to direct us, is still going to be difficult."

"Wow, Mom, that's a lot of stuff to think about."

"Yes, I know. It means this will be a wonderful adventure for us as a family, and it may take more time than I have right now. Think about the time period, generally described, as the Warring States period 476 BCE to 221 BCE. Rob, why don't you look at the books I have by Thomas Cleary—he's an excellent English resource about the Chinese writings. You can also look at my *Huangdi Neijing*, and the *Tao Te Ching*—oh wait, my *Tao Te Ching* is at the office. There may be another one in the bookshelf with the other ones I mentioned. It's an old text, with very old Chinese writing, at the back of the shelf. I found it at an old bookstore in Del Mar, California, years ago. I don't know what it's about, but I loved the lettering. Here it is. It may help. I think I have to go get ready for the next channeling. Love you two! Have fun."

"Bye Mom, love you too."

Rob grabs Sarabeth's arm as she is leaving. He softly kisses Sarabeth's cheek.

"Rest before you go into the channeling. Love you."

Sarabeth touches Rob's shoulder.

"Don't worry, I think I'm doing OK. I'm going to go on a quick run with Leo—that will help me really get centered and grounded."

Sarabeth quickly hugs Sophia and walks into the room across the hall. She changes into her running clothes. Her thoughts return to the texts she was looking at, and she realizes that there may be another good book on lettering in her study. She takes her shoes into her study and looks at her bookshelf. She reminisces about her time in Del Mar, and the huge Torrey Pines and the ocean. Sarabeth strokes a frog netsuke in her palm as she searches her bookshelf. *I bet it has the right writing for Sophia's dream*, she thinks to herself. *I'll have to look later tonight after the channeling, when I'm less distracted.* She puts on her shoes quickly and leaves the room.

CHAPTER 4

uman behavior flows from three main sources: desire (intent), emotion (sense), and knowledge (intellect). ... First there is the archetype of form, a priori, and then there is the creation of the seen archetype, tangible form, a posteriori...Form is created first as internal vision of the phenomenon and second as the physical phenomenon.

—Plato

A sensible man will remember that the eyes can be confused in two ways – by a change from light to darkness or from darkness to light; and he will recognize the same thing happens to the soul... Whereas our argument shows that the power and capacity of learning exists in the soul already; and just as the eye was unable to turn from darkness to light without the whole body, so too the instrument of knowledge can only by the movement of the whole soul be turned from the world of becoming into that of being...How could they see anything but the shadows if they were never allowed to move their heads...Escape from the limitations of the cave offers the opportunity to discover true reality with a final, almost mystical awareness of goodness as the origin (source) of everything.

—Plato, the Allegory of the Cave

The late afternoon winds are beginning to pick up, and it feels very refreshing inside Sarabeth's study. Revived from her run, she gathers some extra items to bring with her to the living room as she prepares to go into a channeled state.

Debbie and Jan are returning from their afternoon walk, laughing and looking at the pottery they found at the dirt mound. As they walk in the front door, they see Bob and

Peter in the living room, talking. Debbie shows her arrowhead to Bob.

"Look at what we found at the dig. Really cool pottery shards, and I even found an arrowhead made out of obsidian. It's extraordinary. I think you would love to excavate there too. We can go tomorrow if you want. How has your visit been, you two?"

"Very nice, actually," Peter responds. "Jan, I'm surprised you took any pottery from the site. Did you ask permission of the pieces to take them with you?"

"I absolutely did, Peter," Jan answers gently. "I felt these pieces were ready to come with me and teach me about the energy of the space before it was a ruin. I sensed there was a sweetness to them that I was supposed to incorporate into my work."

Peter touches the small shards and smiles at Jan. "Good, then."

"I think we have more questions than answers from our discussion, so that is exhilarating," Bob says.

Debbie laughs.

"Well, good. I think we need to get ready for the channeling, right?"

"Yes." Jan says. "Come with me, Peter."

Peter gets up slowly and waves to Debbie and Bob.

"See you in a few. Great talking to you Bob, more later."

Jan and Peter slowly walk down the hallway to their room.

Debbie and Bob get their stuff and leave the living room. Bob thinks about his conversation with Peter as Debbie talks about the pottery shards.

"I think this this place is an energy vortex, we just go a few steps away and it's like we are in a different world. What a treasure!"

Just then, Debbie sees Laurel standing at the end of the hallway. It seems as if she is in the middle of something—almost like she was coming out of their room rather than her own. Her energy feels like she is caught, but Debbie brushes the thought aside.

"Hi Laurel. How are you doing? We just got back from the big dirt mound, which I'm now referring to as the dig. Look at all the pottery shards I found."

"Oh, hi you guys." Laurel says as she unconsciously shifts her weight, brushing aside what was in her mind. "Yes, Sophia and I found some stuff there too. It is like a dig. What are you two doing?"

"I think it's time to get ready for the next channeling." Bob responds.

"OK, well, I better change then. Um, well, see you later." Laurel quickly darts into her room.

Debbie turns to Bob. "Well, that was a little weird, don't you think?"

"What? Laurel? Well, yes, her energy did seem off, but she is a bit of an odd duck, so maybe that's normal for her."

"I guess you're right. But it seemed to me that she was actually exiting our room, not her own, and that we just kind of caught her in the act. But why would she be in our room?"

"Hmm, are you sure? You think she was actually in our room? There isn't really anything in there. Just our clothes and books and stuff."

"Yes, I know. I think I'll ask Sarabeth about it anyway."

"OK, but don't start a fuss, honey, especially if there isn't anything missing."

"I know, but it's weird."

Bob hugs Debbie gently to comfort her, and then goes into the bathroom to wash up. Debbie looks around the room, trying to discern what might have been of interest to Laurel. "Why would she be in our room... " Debbie mumbles under her breath. Finally, she goes outside to sit on the side patio. She takes a few cleansing breaths, quietly centering her energy. She uses the natural environment to help her: the low hum of the cars, a hummingbird as it feeds on the flowers in the tree next to her, the sensation of the sun on her face. She releases her anxiety and relaxes.

She hears Bob in the background say, "OK, we'll be right there." She comes in and quickly changes her clothes and washes her face.

"I'm ready dear, are you?"

"Yes, let's go and join the others," Bob says as he gathers Debbie's hand and clasps it. "Don't worry, we'll discover what's going on."

As they exit, Debbie and Bob bump right into Laurel again.

"Oh, hi…right, well, let's all go join the others."

They all walk down the hallway to the living room.

Already seated are Sophia, Rob, Sarabeth, Jan, and Peter. Sarabeth warmly waves her friends to the empty seats.

"Hi, welcome you three, come in. So, the setup for the channeling is pretty much the same each time. Remember, you can get quite dizzy sometimes, especially if you join in the frequency upleveling, so don't forget to use your personal methods to ground yourself. The chocolate, peanut butter energy bars, and water are still out and available to you.

"Because today has been filled with a lot of activity, I want to focus our intention on what we want to experience and receive from the channeling. Bring your attention into this space right here, right now. Please, take a deep, cleansing breath and release all the day's activities as you exhale. With the next breath, imagine that you are bringing in golden light into the top of your head and it is moving down through your body, along your spine, and then out your feet and hands. As you exhale, release any nagging negative energy, feeling, or physical symptom. Now, with your third breath, imagine yourself fully and completely in this room. Set a loving intention for this channeling."

Sarabeth opens her eyes and looks at her friends in the room. She sees them vibrating, with color and energy around their bodies. Light is going between them and her and connecting to the natural space outside the windows. She sees the webstrings connecting like a tapestry of life. "Wonderful—good work everyone. We are all vibrating at a much higher level and with a sweet connection."

Sarabeth puts a lozenge into her mouth and takes a deep breath as she begins her inner directing mantra. "OK, let's begin:

"Source energy, allow me to be a clear healing channel. I call in one hundred thousand angels to please come in and fill this room. I invite in only high frequency light beings. Please come in, guide me, and offer me interpretation for this second evening of this retreat on healing psycho-emotional trauma through the ancient traditions... Thank you for your protection and guidance dear Archangel Michael, Archangel Gabriel, Metatron, Orion, the Council of Twelve, Archangel Raphael, the Marys, and Archangel Ariel."

Sarabeth feels the voice and words from the channel and begins to simply speak what is presented to her. Her voice lightens, gaining increased softness as she speaks the words as if they are her own but learning the content for the first time as she herself hears the words from her own voice.

"Dearly beloved, we are here and we want you to know how much we love each of you. It is a joy to assist you in bringing increased light into your vessels as you choose to have this experience, make an intention to open further to your healing traditions, and discover more fully how all is energy and light.

"We are grateful for your ongoing focus and attention to the light and the ancient knowledge found within. Integration of spirit, mind, and body are necessary for healing and health. To increase your integration process, allow first to be at peace within, go into your heart center, and open to love. From an open heart center, you are able to receive a higher frequency of light. Anchor this in your field through

intention and connection to source. You may imagine this as a light that moves through your chakra system and anchors into your field.

"Attention and intention focus energy and creation...You create that to which you put your attention. Emotions and feelings are the key. Pay attention to that which brings you joy, that which you desire, and this is what you will create. Pay attention to that which you fear or to that which is lacking, and you create more of that fear and lacking—flip back and forth between the two attentions and you create a stagnation or spiral between. You choose your creation through your attention and intention and love.

"Your emotions are the doorway for you to further understand and connect with frequency. Integration of your spiritual, emotional, and physical bodies increases your capacity to hold the higher frequencies of light on the planet so that you may create healing and change. Through your emotional body you connect to your spiritual body. You may feel you want to avoid unpleasant emotions. However, you must lean into and love your emotions, face each emotion, and feel your way through it.

"Remain open to where the flow of your emotion brings you. Through this method of openness, you will connect to higher and higher frequencies of light. This will allow you to move out of the need or belief that you have to control your emotion. Control has been useful to you as a focus; however, now the idea is to flow though, rather than control. The energies of flow and allowing are key to increasing the frequency of light. Allowing each emotion its expression, with love and compassion, allows for it to be released and you to be guided to your true, essential being. From this space you can go under, deeper, and see what is in your best interest, what is underneath, at the core, and out of a natural inner guidance, be guided by sensefulness through the emotion to what brings you joy.

"First we want to talk about levels of lightbody and the fields or bodies that make up a multidimensional being: you. Then we want to address how to use emotions to access the emotional, spiritual, and mental bodies for the elevation of your consciousness and that of your clients.

"There are 12 levels of lightbody frequencies. The third and fourth levels, also known as the astral level, make up the lower creation realm. This is the realm of duality and karma; here energy is solid and hard. Thought is the way in which you create your world but there are still many people who are unable to get out of their limiting thought patterns and beliefs. The fifth through ninth levels of lightbody make up the mid-creation realm, and the planet is currently ascending out of the mid-astral plane and vibrating at this mid-creation plane. So the planet is ascending out of third and fourth dimension into fifth and sixth dimension. Fifth dimension is the first dimension where you are completely spiritually oriented. Sixth dimension holds light language and uses color and tone. Here you are a dynamic thought, creating as you think and adjusting to hold higher degrees and amounts of light.

You create directly through your consciousness. This is where Sarabeth and some of you are already working, both within your own personal work and with your clients, when focusing on healing limiting thought patterns and beliefs, habit reaction patterns, and moving the energy of the communities in which you work toward a sense of oneness and the unified field of light and energy. Seventh dimension is pure light and pure sacred geometry. It is here where you are connected with infinite refinement. In eighth dimension you begin to experience as one thought your soul group. Ninth dimension is the place of the collective unconscious and the full experience of the unified field. Tenth through twelfth frequencies are the upper creation realm and these we will discuss further in a future channeling. The tenth dimension is that of Elohim and the source of the Rays. This is the high council—a higher vibration of light that is accessed once you have released the sense of individuality and control. The Rays are higher frequencies of light connected to ascended masters. Some of you have experienced information channeling through you from St. Germain and the Violet Ray and Babiji. These energies are healing and allow for immediate miracle creation and deep healing of the human aspect of your soul. When you call on or experience this communication, you see the strength of love, your heart center, and soul path. This extinguishes the need to be driven by fear and anger, revenge, and other secondary human personality and drives. The eleventh is the realm of Metatron, the archangels, and the Akashic Records. The twelfth is the all, the one point, the experience of all as one point. In this dimension you are able to see and be a light glowing within the tapestry of life not only on the planet but with the cosmos. Here you experience a telepathic and sensefulness of all that is.

"You have several bodies that surround you and these are experienced differently in different realms. The physical body uses the physical senses to experience a disconnect from source and separation from the unified field of light, and limitation, the dualistic rather than unification of the divine; This is most dominant in the third and fourth dimensions. The etheric body surrounds the physical body. You experience this about a half-inch away from your skin. This can be accessed as wei qi in Chinese medicine and through polarity. Your etheric body contains your soul blueprint. This informs your multidimensional system about your soul purpose.

"The fifth dimensional aspect of the etheric blueprint is made up of an axiotonal meridian system. The lines of this system are connected through small whorls of electromagnetic energy made up of light and sound and lie along the surface of your skin and the acupuncture meridians, creating a grid of energy that hums along and around your body into a grid for cellular regeneration. The work you are doing in increasing the amount of light you carry turns on this etheric body and awakens you through intuition and meditation to your soul purpose—and when awakened and energized, it assists in lengthened life and intensified life force. You may begin to glow with energy as you excite this system and fill your cells with light. This body dictates how the physical body interprets the information presented to it from the astral, mental, emotional, and spiritual bodies. These bodies surround the physical body and are made up of double tetrahedrons that spin at different rates.

"When you meditate, focus on Metatron's cube to assist in the development and lighting up of this system. The astral body is connected to the fourth dimensional field and the experience of karma. Prior to light activation, the experience of the environment around a being is completely fourth-dimensional patterning, karmic patterning, a stuck loop that the being experiences as limitation and discomfort. In this state you experience repeated patterns of lack, disempowerment, and a sense of victimhood, or emotional or physical illness. These stuck points are like blocks that throw you out of your heart center and drive action toward these less enlightened and fear-based, limited-resource beliefs. These blocks can be shifted through the acupuncture meridians, the axiotonal grid on your body, and opening in the etheric blueprint. The concept of enlightenment is to escape the fourth dimensional karmic loop through light activation into the fifth dimensional blueprint. The mental body determines how you create reality through thought. This is enhanced and directed by the integration of the interaction of the emotional and spiritual bodies toward increased mindfulness and sensefulness, which allows more light to activate this integrated system. Through these bodies you feel and express your experience of reality and create your truth.

"So, emotion and thought directed through the spiritual and etheric bodies are how each human being creates the physical body and experience in reality. The process of intention and attention focus these bodies and you can use the whorls of energy that lie along the acupuncture meridians to access cell regeneration and activation of higher levels of consciousness.

"The continuum of control and allowing is connected to creation and ownership in your soul-directed life path. Development of habitual dissonances in your behavior in order to avoid pain or in reaction to what you call anxiety, which we see as 'not living,' is a skewing out away from your essential being and soul purpose, or life path. It is like holding your breath, blocking the flow in inspiration and expiration of energy so that your self becomes bound and small. This energetic action is what creates all disease in your spirit, mind, and body.

"All disease begins from the perspective of 'shen," from a spiritual disconnect within a being. This begins in the fourth dimension of energy and light: The Astral dimension. From there, it can develop into distorted thinking, misbeliefs which, over time, distort the energetic flow around you and create stagnation and *visceral distortion, and lead to holding and blocking of energy, which results in disease in the physical body and drives maladaptive thinking and behavior. You can become so disconnected from source you may take actions that are extremely negative to your soul or that of another. You block the light frequency available to you and create a dulling of your senses and a distortion of your perceptions. Over time, like a pipe that gets clogged from garbage buildup, the energetic pulsing gets stagnant and clogged. This is exacerbated by behaviors that dull the precise working of the physical body, such as lack of quality whole foods and fresh clean water, insufficient exercise, too much exercise, too much sexual activity, a lack of sexual release, a lack of breath through a lack of meditative focus, or inhalant of smoke and pollution. Excess and insufficiency create dissonance in the balance within, and therefore dull the capacity for light and lead to disease within each person. Shock and trauma to the spiritual, emotional, physical system that goes unabated, or which is not worked through so that integration and clearance can be assimilated, leads to disease within the physical, emotional, and spiritual well-being of a being. In some traditions this is called 'soul retrieval,' where an aspect of you has broken off or left so that your overall vitality dims.*

"Healing of such trauma comes from the release of the original trauma, and the return of that aspect of your soul lost in response to the trauma. We see this occurring through a shift in focus of attention and intention, and a direct connection to light through the experience, meditation, and self-love, or a sacred healing ceremony with a more connected light being. Loving oneself fully and experiencing forgiveness heals. When the trauma is reworked from this perspective and the lost aspects of the soul are returned, you are freer to choose different ways of being in your life that are directed by your fifth-dimensional blueprint. Using attention and intention and your emotions as a guide, these stagnating and harmful patterns can be eliminated. This requires flexibility, focus, and flow. Extinguishing the controlling patterns developed to assuage the pain, fear, and anxiety also assist in the release of the trauma, a return to balance, and an opening to love

and forgiveness. *These mechanisms work in unison in the spiritual, emotional, and physical bodies.*

"This will be the continued focus of the next few offerings. We are aware that you have questions and would like to answer these to your completion. Archangel Ariel, Archangel Raphael, Orion, and the Council of Twelve have offered insights in this channeling, and many high light beings are ready to provide loving guidance and information for you. We want you to know how much we love you and how grateful we are to be your interpreters for this information.

"We are available for specific questions...remember to drink plenty of water to help you at the cellular level as you are integrating this information and increasing the degree and frequency of light you are each holding. Cleanse your energy field with lavender and sage as well as palo santos. Allow yourselves plenty of rest to help with assimilation of this information. Use the grounding foods. You may use cleansing baths that incorporate baking soda and sea salt, or hot oil treatments so you may be grounded through touch. Salt on the balls of your feet will assist the anchoring of the light and new information.

"We are so pleased to have this opportunity to share this information. We love you very much...We await any questions you may have."

Sarabeth lightly speaks.

"Thank you so much, Archangel Ariel, The Council of Twelve, Orion, Archangel Raphael, Metatron, the Marys, and Sirius. I am so grateful for this information. At this time, I will open it up to questions. Please begin from my left."

Peter speaks in a hushed voice.

"Hello. Can you talk about the issue of creation more fully? How does thinking something create it, and how can shifting your thinking shift the energetic and substantial quality of the world?"

"This is an idea that can be both enlightening and a bottleneck for human beings. Creation happens twice: first in the thought of it, the imagination process, and then in the substance of the thing. So what we are saying is, if you can think it, you can create it—or, more

to the point: *Upon thinking it, it is. This is where clarity becomes important as well as light and love as frequencies. The power to create is awesome. It is. It is within each being. As a person focuses and clarifies his internal guidance through love and light, he is then able to create a higher level of awareness and increased energy toward his essential, soul life path, so creating prosperity is a simple process of seeing it, aligning with it in love and light, and then seeing it in the physical. For this to happen at the 'speed of light', or what you might call a miracle, the person must be free of misbeliefs or habitual patterns that say this isn't so. It is through the knowing that this is so, so that one sees and experiences the immediate shift in consciousness and experience. This is the deep experience of how your perception of the world defines it and creates your reality. The idea that what you believe is what you see.*

"Clarifying yourself through meditation, prayer, healthy eating, lack of ingestion of harmful substances, sufficient exercise for your body type, efficient rest, and self-love allows for the removal and release of these incorrect misbeliefs about your power. The use of ancient ceremonial plant medicines can be helpful for those clinging to misbeliefs or stuck in a cycle of desire for and resistance to change. Your thinking is connected to your being—emotional and spiritual and physical being—and when you are distorted within this integration, your thinking is distorted. This is an interactive system. Each affects the other. You can heal your thinking through reclamation of healthful living, cleansing your physical actions and behaviors with a focus on prayer and/or meditation, or you can heal you body through shifting your thinking through meditation, paradigm shifting, perspective clarification, prayer, self-love, and loving-kindness. The tradition of yoga—all aspects of this tradition, not just the asanas—utilizes these processes to create health, and this is a way to focus on self-love and to release unwanted, non-useful beliefs and physical holding patterns, so that you can focus on increasing the level of light you can hold within your physical body. Does this answer your question, Peter?"

"Yes, yes, thank you very much."

Peter sits back, continuing to rapidly write down the information.

Sophia begins to speak. "Mom, may I ask one more question?"

"Yes, honey."

"Hi, this is Sophia. I wanted to know why so many people aren't willing to open to the love and light frequencies. Why can't they see it? Is there a way to show it to them?"

"Hello Sophia, this is a very sweet question from you. We first want you to know that we are aware that you have come to the planet as part Rainbow star-seed to assist not only your beloved parents, but also the global environment of your planet to uplevel. We see that you see what is, and are frustrated that those around you, your peers, and your teachers, do not. This frustration is something that can get in your way from connecting fully to the light. We want you to understand that it is each being's choice to connect to the light. The Pleiadians often share about your planet being a 'free-will zone,' so that each person may come to their level of light through their attention and intention, and inner guidance. This does not mean that you have to stop creating opportunities to provide information about light and love and energy and consciousness to others. This is part of your essential being to do so. Be willing to allow the receiver of the information to do with it what best suits her. Release an inner need to make her understand. Simply offer freely the truth from your whole being, and then release responsibility for the other's understanding of that truth. Does this answer your question?"

"Yes, I guess so. Thank you."

She looks sadly at her mother.

"Be at peace little one, all is well. Love to all present, remember to ground."

Peter looks over at Sarabeth.

"Can I ask a follow-up question?

"Of course. I am holding up well. Go ahead."

Peter quietly begins to formulate the question as he speaks. "So, uh, the whorls of energy that are part of the etheric body, those are the acupuncture points, right? So, are there actual combinations of points that help to move through the different levels of light?"

"Yes, as you know from your training, this information was blocked by the development of TCM. However, some information does still exist about which points are most useful and when, especially within the Lingshu Jing. The ghost points and windows of the sky points in proper combinations as well as other specific points along the gallbladder and du channels assist in activation of the fourth eye, which helps you connect and open to the information in the etheric body through your causal chakra and causal body that surrounds your etheric body. You remember that Sarabeth could feel emotion in the pulses, and that she focused often on the jing river points? This was information that was part of her DNA and connection with Archangel Ariel; as you meditate on these and focus your intention and attention, you will see these lighten and vibrate so you will know which to use when. Is this helpful?"

Peter stops furiously writing and looks at Sarabeth.

"Oh, yes. Thank you."

Sarabeth gently wipes tears from her eyes.

"Thank you, all high light beings, for your support and your information today. Each of you is of great benefit. Thank you all. Archangel Michael, if you could clear the energy, thank you, thank you. Kadosh, kadosh, kadosh. Om mani padme hum. Om, gam, Ganapataye, namaha."

"OK everyone, how are you doing? We were pretty high in the light frequency; I know I'm feeling a bit dizzy."

Sarabeth drinks some water and puts a lozenge into her mouth.

"Please everyone, before we get up to walk around, drink the water at your places and perhaps have some peanut butter energy bars or a piece of chocolate."

Sophia goes over to sit with Sarabeth and hugs her. Peter is still writing, and Jan and Debbie are quietly meditating.

Rob, Bob, and Laurel are talking quietly together about the information.

"One theme that keeps returning is this issue of self-love and going within for inner guidance," Laurel says to Rob and Bob.

"Yes, it is a recurrent theme. The question is how to get the general population to do this," Bob says with an overriding sense of discouragement. "So often in society, individuals look to others for guidance and proper action and ignore that which they intuit and sense from within."

"I think the idea is to show others through our actions," Rob says. "So we need to have faith, be in faith, and trust that the light frequency and love energy will shift the perspectives of those around us, naturally, and with a certainty that can shift the whole consciousness. Pretty awesome concept: to live the truth and through our living it, it transforms the energy, like it amps the level of light. *It is.* That is what keeps ringing in my ears: '*It is.*' So powerful!"

Rob feels really energized as he gets up and crosses the room to Sarabeth.

"Beautiful, honey, truly beautiful!"

He kisses her and Sophia.

"See you later. I want to do some painting."

"I think I'm going to go out to our 'dig' and do some meditation," Laurel calls into the group.

"Oh, I want to join you," Debbie says as she starts to join Laurel. "I have something I really want to talk with you about."

Out of the corner of her ear, Sarabeth takes in the conversation with Debbie and Laurel. Immediately her mind goes back to Laurel's mother's death and Laurel's comments at the beginning of the retreat; she nervously shifts in her chair. As an uncontrollable shiver runs through her she feels an overwhelming sense of doom.

"Mom, are you OK?" Sophia looks at her mother. "Why are you shivering?"

"Oh honey, it's nothing. Do you want to get some food with me?"

"Yes, I'm hungry. Let's go."

Debbie is walking at a fast pace to keep up with Laurel, who seems to be trying to get away from her and distracted by something.

"Did you hear what Rob said? He seemed so energized and pumped, like the channel was speaking directly to him. 'Trust' and 'it is.' I thought that was a powerful piece of information too. What do you think, Laurel?"

"Oh, I think it was a great piece of information. I'm just thinking about something else I wanted to ask the channel but didn't feel ready to yet. I've been bothered by something a long time and I feel I am about to discover the answer, but I'm hesitant to find the truth. It's weird. That whole thing about living the truth and the truth heals; it's a lot to really hold in your head at once. You know what I mean? Perhaps I haven't been focused on the right things and that's why I can't discover the truth I'm searching to find. It's really bothering me, trying to make sense out of it."

Debbie looks at Laurel quizzically.

"Laurel, I don't think I know what you're talking about. I feel like I'm missing a very important piece of information."

"Me too. That's the whole point!"

Debbie, still confused, decides to talk about something else.

"So, Laurel, I was wondering if you could talk with someone who has died for me. Do you think you could try to contact her for me? I have something to kind of work out with her." Debbie's voice trails off as she sees an amazing piece of pottery sticking up out of the earth. "Wow, how could this be here in such good condition? I don't understand."

Laurel smiles.

"I know. It's such a treat, isn't it? It's like a real archeological dig, and they are so nonchalant about it. They're so funny. Sarabeth has always loved rocks and fossils. Have you seen all the petrified wood she has found? It's crazy! And she's always coming across some treasure—even the other day when she was running with Leo on the same path thousands of others run and she uses almost daily, she came across this rock that had probably 10 fossils in it. She ran all the way home holding it. It's like the ancient earth is drawn to her."

Both women try to pull the large pottery piece out of the mound very carefully. While leaning in toward Laurel, Debbie asks, "So, do you think you would be willing to help me talk with my old friend?"

Startled at Debbie's gentle and wistful demeanor, Laurel looks into Debbie's eyes. "Uh, yeah sure—I mean, if I can connect with her." Laurel feels a shudder down her neck and pulls away from Debbie's field.

"Hey, you can have the pottery piece, I think I'm going to go back."

Laurel turns away without waiting for any response from Debbie, and quickly walks off.

Debbie, a little bewildered, lightly calls after Laurel, "OK, we can talk later." Turning her attention to the piece, Debbie remarks to herself, "Well, that was odd." She pulls the piece out of the mound and smiles at it. As she walks away she notices another piece: This one is shiny and looks sharp. It's an obsidian arrowhead. She grabs it, smiling. Then she walks back slowly to the house.

Sarabeth notices Laurel retuning.

"Hey Laurel, you OK? You don't look OK."

"Yeah, I'm OK. I had this strange talk with Debbie. I feel like I know who she wants to contact, and it's making me anxious. How would I know the person? I don't remember meeting Debbie before. Hey, how did you guys meet? Is there some connection that I don't know about between her and me?"

Sarabeth looks at Laurel with gentleness. She can feel she is disturbed.

"I don't think so. I met Debbie and Bob through my work, way after I knew you, and I don't think either one of them are from here. Who does she want to contact?"

"I don't know. She didn't tell me."

"OK, I'm confused. You just said you thought you knew the person. ...How do you think that if you don't know who it is?"

"It's something in how she asked me. I was standing really close to her and could see-feel into her field and eyes. It made me sense the person, and it felt like I knew her. It kind of scared and excited me all at once—too much, I think. I freaked out, honestly. I had to leave."

"Wow, cool! Now I'm curious about who it is. I have to say, earlier, I was feeling a little weird when you left together. I think there's something in this that we're missing. I mean, other than the person's name."

"Yeah, I think you're right. I also think I'm not quite ready to find that missing piece."

CHAPTER 5

T he golden flower parallels the circular mandala, which represents the mystery at the center of being, a journey to self; these processes parallel psyche development...The psyche possesses a common substratum transcending all differences in culture and consciousness, the collective unconscious...The various lines of psychic development start from one common stock whose roots reach back into all strata of the past...It means that mankind has common instincts of imagination and of action. And all conscious imagination and action have been developed with these unconscious archetypal images as their basis, and always remain bound to them.

—Carl Jung, The Secret of the Golden Flower

At the center of the Hui Ming Ching, The Book of Consciousness and Life, is the Tao, the way. That which exists through itself is called the way. The subtlest secret of the Tao is human nature and life...Meditation on the Secret of the Golden Flower assists to bring you to your center and the Tao.

—Carl Jung, commentary on Hui Ming Ching

Dreams offer archetypes of the collective unconscious to the dreamer for resolution and integration.

—Carl Jung, Man and His Symbols

Sophia is rifling through her mother's Chinese texts trying to find actual Chinese lettering. She hopes it will spark a reaction to help her remember more of her dream. "I wish Mom would help me with this. She knows so much more about this than I do," Sophia mutters to herself.

"Mom, will you come in and help me with something? I'm in Dad's studio...please...Mom!" Sophia yells.

Quickly, Sarabeth enters the studio. "Sophia, are you OK?"

"Yes, but I was wondering if you would help me find the right time period for my dream through the correct Chinese lettering. I really think there's something important in my dream that relates to what you're talking about in your channeling interpretations." Sophia stops what she's doing and looks at Sarabeth with a very serious gaze.

"OK, honey, what have you done so far to pin down the time period?"

"Well, first I looked at the Warring States period like you said, but none of your books about the Yellow Emperor have any Chinese lettering. So then I just started looking at all of your Chinese philosophy books."

Sarabeth looks at all of her books lying on Rob's drawing table. "Well, that doesn't seem to be working. Perhaps we should try a computer search?"

Sarabeth walks out of the studio, gets her laptop from her study, and returns.

"So, can you tell me what the lettering looked like? What do you remember from your dream?"

Sophia looks at her mother with a frown.

"No, Mom, that's the problem—I can't remember. I was hoping that seeing the lettering would help me."

"OK, let's see what we get online. I'm going to look for images that may help. OK, here it is. Does this look like what you saw in your dream?"

"It sort of does, but the characters looked more 'flowery'—like the difference between handwriting and printing. This looks more like printing, but in the dream the lettering was more 'flowery.'"

"But in general it feels like this is the correct lettering?"

"Yes, I think so. When is it?"

"Well, this lettering is part of the Warring States Period—but that's a long period of time, from 476 BCE to 221 BCE. I think we need to search to see if there were changes within that period to determine a more specific date."

Sarabeth continues to click on different pages, looking at the information until she finds a page with a chart on it.

"Honey, look at these different characters for the same word—which of these looks most like the ones in your dream?"

Sophia studies the characters.

"Mom, I think this is it—do you see how it curls up there? I remember a character that looked like that. I think this is it!" Sophia exclaimed, jumping up and down. She's pointing to an old manuscript that was used as an example of a specific kind of writing from the Han Warring States Period.

Sarabeth looked at the image and then went back to read about the script. "So, it appears it's called 'proto-clerical evolving to clerical,' and it is during 'the beginning of the Han Period' that is following the Qin Period, so just following the Warring States Period, I think. So, after 221 BCE through the middle of Emperor Wu of the Western Han's reign, which was from 141 BCE to 87 BCE. Very interesting. It looks like it actually developed out of Vulgar Qin writing, although I do not know what that is."

"I know, so now we have a time period right?" Sophia asked.

"Yes, honey, but now we have to try to see if we can, through reading the history of the time, get a sense about who the potential actors are in your dream. Remember that during that time only clerics, scribes, and nobleman would write. Although it looks like the article says there was also something called 'vulgar' writing, which would indicate that businesspeople could also write."

Sarabeth's voice trails off as she continues to read from the computer.

"OK, look at this."

Sarabeth points to a picture and some information about the ruling leader during that time. "I wonder if it's this family that you dreamed about. This is very interesting, Sophia. What a wonderful adventure mystery! Read these three links and then let me know what you think with respect to your dream. I'm going to try to make a chart to identify how this family and the characters are linked, and if there is any connection between the information about love and light energy and this family's history. What fun, dear."

Sarabeth gently hugs Sophia and, moving away some of her books from Rob's drawing table, she grabs a clean piece of drawing paper and starts writing down the names and time periods as well as interesting notes about the ruling family.

"Mom, let's put the computer here so we can both reference it. I'm going to bookmark the pages so we won't lose them as we go back and forth. This is fun!"

Sophia, sitting next to Sarabeth, takes a different sheet of notebook paper and starts writing notes about how the information correlates with her dream. All of a sudden she looks at one of the pictures.

"Mom, I think this is one of the men in my dream...I can't tell for sure, but I think it is. It's like the channel said, I can feel-know something about the face represented here."

"Sophia, are you sure? I don't know how accurate these drawings are to what the people actually looked like—it's not like the pictures we take today, you know."

"I know, Mom, but there's something about it that is familiar. The channel said we should trust those inner knowings, right? So I think it means something—his name is Liu Ruyi. This is so cool. It says that he was the son, fourth son, of Emperor Gao or Gaozu of Han, and his mother was

Concubine Qi. He was Prince of Dai and Prince Yin of Zhao. Oh, Mom, he was assassinated by his brother's mother. How amazing! It fits with the dream, except there's nothing about his writings. And he didn't have any children, so who am I in the dream? More questions! But it's fun to get on the trail with some answers. How exciting, Mom! I'm going to do some more research on his dad, the emperor, and his brother, and brother's mom."

Sophia starts to search between the links, completely lost in the information. Sarabeth looks lovingly at her and pats her on the arm as she works.

"OK, honey, I have to prepare for the interpretation. Maybe you can come up with some questions for the channel tonight to get more clarification about why the dream came to you? Love you!"

Sophia barely responds. "Yeah, OK, see you later Mom, love you too."

Sarabeth walks out of the studio and goes into her study to prepare for the channeling. She hears Rob and Peter in the living room, discussing the issue of how disruption in shen and emotional or spiritual energy causes disease. Rob is talking about toning as a tool for shen disorder.

"Sarabeth studied the use of tuning forks to connect with tone and sound to redirect the energy to *a priori*. It was amazing to watch when she practiced toning through the different sounds. I could see her vibrate into a stronger vessel. We used this method with Sophia when she was really young. It was such a powerful tool. Since her spiritual connection was still so strong, she had immediate reconsolidation. It helped with teething, insomnia, and just fussiness; and it was such a simple thing. I'm certain that's what was originally behind lullabies: how the sound and tone of a mother's voice brought about the concordance of the spirit, mind, and body channels to bring about integrated harmony. Over time, the reason behind the sounds and toning was lost and the words were thought to be important, but that was after the mind was given such a strong position in how things were interpreted. It was such a misstep in focus. Harmony and integration has to come first from the sensory guidance system, and then the mind follows suit—not the other way around. I think this is what the channel was trying to get to this last time."

"Rob, that is fascinating. What a great theory to test whether sound heals and how various sounds are healing, and under what conditions. Was it always the same? I mean, what sound Sophia needed. Or did it change as she grew or from circumstance to circumstance? What data did you collect?"

"Peter, you are such an interesting thinker! Well, I'm not sure I collected any data, but I do think that different circumstances required different sounds; I think Sarabeth used different tones for different symptoms. She used a lot of songs from *The Sound of Music*. I always thought that was because it was a set of songs she knew from her own childhood, but she once told me that the songs hit all the tones she needed for the various concerns that Sophia had. She said the 'Do-Re-Mi' song was especially helpful because it hit specific notes that corresponded with the natural sounds she studied from one of her teachers in something she called Inochi Medicine, and Shinto. The sounds correspond with eh, ee, ah, o, oo, which connect with the five elements and five spirits to align the body and mind with spirit. This was useful to consolidate qi and resonate with an integrated spirit, mind, and body energy connection. She thought the popularity of a lot of songs had to do with this underlying healing harmony rather than the words, and that is why she noted that people liked songs even when they did not know the words or learned the words incorrectly. There have been a number of studies regarding the healing aspect of tuning forks. I bet there is a lot of data with that. Aspects of Japanese

Shinto medicine utilizes toning and sound in a specific way too. Did you study Japanese techniques in your training?"

"I didn't, but I had a good friend who did, and he used to talk about *a priori* and *a posteriori* in this same way that *a priori* was from spirit or a spiritual perfect state, and *a posteriori* was what was on the planet, after science and mind got into the picture. He would try to find the one, single acupuncture point that acted like a toning and reset the energy system in the body to *a priori*. It was fascinating to watch him work and often he was very successful in doing this. His original training was highly affected by the idea of sound and toning."

"I know that Sarabeth uses her toning bowls and also tuning forks as she works with acupuncture points. She says that it is very useful for strengthening and aligning the Wei Qi, or warrior energy, around the body. She seems to also use it with the extraordinary channel-opening points when she is working with psychiatric issues or complicated toxicity issues, soul retrieval, and trauma. She says these all derive from spirit or shen disorder or disconnect due to trauma, injury, stress, or loss. It seems to act like a pathway for soul retrieval and reset of the integrated energy system."

"Rob, that's an interesting next level of treatment to work at the energy level through sound. I'm going to start using this. Are there any guides for the use of toning, or is it just through intuition?"

"Well, from what I've seen it looks like a lot of it is intuitive, but I do think there is a guide. Let's go upstairs and see if I can find it in Sarabeth's books."

Rob gets up and starts walking toward the stairs.

"This is really exciting talking with you about this, Peter. I'm sorry it's taken so long for us to connect!"

Peter follows Rob up the steps.

"I agree, Rob! We have a lot in common, and I enjoy your perspective on things."

As they walk up the stairs, they see Sarabeth in her study quietly meditating. Rob puts his finger to his lips and looks at Peter. He points to the door opposite the stairs and walks across the hall into his study, motioning Peter to follow.

"Wow, Rob, this is an amazing studio! Hi, Sophia!"

"Hi, Dad! Hi, Peter! I'm working on my dream. I think we found the guy I saw get killed in my dream. Like it was a real thing, I think. Isn't that exciting?"

Sophia grabs her dad's arm and pulls him toward her page of dates and information.

"Look, Dad, isn't this cool? This is the guy. I think I found him. Now I have to see what the dream was trying to tell me, and why I had the dream anyway. This is so cool."

Rob pats Sophia on her back.

"Good job, Sophia! Did your Mom help you or did you figure this out on your own?"

Rob then notices all the books strewn on his drawing table.

"Wow, you really went through everything, didn't you?"

He starts to bring the books back to their shelves.

"Dad, I'll put them back—I just wanted to get to a good stopping point. Mom helped me find the right time period, and this is the Chinese writing that we found. It really looks like what I saw in my dream. Peter, are you good at dreams like Debbie and Bob?"

Peter smiles at Rob and Sophia.

"Wow, you really have a great adventure here. No, Sophia, that's not one of my specialties. In fact, I'm not quite sure I understand what you're trying to discover here."

"Oh, I'm sorry Peter, I guess you were meditating when I talked about this yesterday. I had a dream about a Chinese nobleman I witnessed being killed, and when he was killed, the person that killed him stole all of his writings. I saw the writing in my dream, and I knew what it meant while

I was asleep, but now I don't. I'm trying to make sense of the dream because I think it has an important message for me or us about the channelings. Dad was helping me earlier, but we didn't get very far. But now I think I've found him. See, that's him, in the drawing on the computer. His name is Liu Ruyi and his dad was the Emperor of Gao or Gaozu of the Western Han, and his brother was Emperor Wu, and his brother's mother had him killed. The thing is, I don't know how it relates to the channeling on healing psycho-emotional issues. I know it does, but I don't know how."

"Well, Sophia, I don't know very much about dreams, but I do know a lot about Chinese history and Chinese medicine. And there is something very interesting about this family; I may know why you dreamed that dream. There are some myths about a very important document that was written during that particular time that had to do with reconnecting to spirit, but that it was lost. It has to do with Liu Ruyi's father, the Emperor Gao. He was not very learned or scholarly when he was young. In fact, he was kind of a playboy. The myth begins with him being born under a dragon cloud, and when he got into trouble the cloud was always there, just above him. This was an ominous sign, and he always had very good fortune. After he won a very important battle that landed him the Emperor of China, he began to take his role more seriously. He was a very generous and kind ruler. And, in fact, he seemed to grow into his role as he matured. He followed the writings of Confucius. Do you know who Confucius is?"

"Yes. Well, I know the *I Ching*. I use it sometimes to guide my day. Mom gave it to me and she said it was Confucian. Is that right?"

"Yes! Very good, Sophia! Well, Emperor Gao became a very strong believer and follower of Confucianism once he became a leader. He followed the theory of the *I Ching*, moral virtue, and the natural law of heaven and earth, in how he ruled, and he was very beloved during his reign because he was kind and fair. One of the stories I read indicated that Emperor Gaozu was such a strong believer that he refused medical treatment from his physician because he believed that heaven had been the benefactor of his success in life, and what would happen in death was heaven's decision."

"By heaven he means God or spirit, right?"

"Sort of. He means the universe or source, which you can interpret to mean God or spirit. And that may be what the writing that was lost was concerning. It was said that this man, his fourth son, Liu Ruyi, was the son of his favorite companion, Concubine Qi, and that he wanted to have him ascend the throne—not Liu Ruyi's brother, Liu Ying, who ultimately became Emperor Hu. Liu Ying was his first wife's son, and she had a lot of power, and she endeavored to both have her son ascend the throne and to have Liu Ruyi killed. What's interesting about your dream is that Liu Ruyi might have been the author of the text that was lost about how to align with and stay in alignment with heaven, spirit or God. It makes sense because of Gaozu's attachment and fondness for this boy and his attraction to Confucianism as he aged. What an amazing journey on which you have embarked. Great work, Sophia!"

"Thanks, Peter, but really you're the person who has shown me the best piece of the puzzle! I am searching for a treatise on light and heaven. Now I just have to figure out how to ask the channel about this, and how I fit into all of it. How come you know so much about this family? I mean, why did you study this particular time?"

"It was an accident, really. I was trying to find the threads of Confucianism in the different time periods. This was a strong resurgence of it, so I did a lot of digging into this family and their relationship to Confucianism. I'm glad I did because it really helps with the mystery of your dream."

Peter reached over to Sophia's paper and started looking at her notes.

"These are very good. May I see the lettering of the time? And let's look at Liu Ruyi's picture again. Maybe something will spark in your memory about your dream so we can know where to look for the lost manuscript."

Rob leaned into the table.

"Sophia, what is this information about here?"

"Oh, that's a chart of the different script of Chinese characters at different times. That's how I first identified the right Chinese writing so that Mom and I could search for information about the time period. It's this one, Dad. See how it's kind of flowery but not like the later period—where it is really flowery? And then see this one, how it's kind of the printed style of the one that fits? The writing that Liu Ruyi was doing was like that middle one, and that fits with the time period when he was actually alive."

"Well, that is amazing." Rob hugs Sophia. "I'm wondering if we can actually ask to talk with him through the channeling. Maybe he could then give us the text that was written by him? I mean verbally tell us, and then we wouldn't have to try to find where it was hidden after it was stolen."

"That's a great idea, Dad. Let's do that. What do you think, Peter?"

"A splendid idea, to be sure. It would be a real treasure to have that information to use in our studies and practice."

CHAPTER 6

The great Tao of the gold elixir is first found through calm stability. If you are not calm and stable, your spirit and will are confused and disorderly; even if you tune the true breath, the breath will not remain, so the true energy cannot enter...Only through calm, stable breathing meditation and visualization of golden light can you maintain the true breath.

Then with your true spirit, convey your true energy to permeate your whole body evenly...the positive energy has been attained and the passes can be opened...thus the three treasures of vitality, energy, and spirit experience a daily flourishing of life and fill the whole body, so that the great medicine can be expected to be produced naturally.

—Chang Po-Tuan, The Secret of Opening the Passes

The three passes are the critical junctures of the three fundamentals: vitality, energy, and spirit. The body unmoving, refining vitality into energy, rising through the coccyx, is called the first pass. The mind unmoving, refining energy into spirit, stopping at midspine is called the middle pass. The intent unmoving, refining spirit into spaciousness, rising to the back of the skull, is called the upper pass. When body, mind, and intent merge into one, the vitality energy and spirit meet without excitement or disharmony; this is the seed of the gold elixir.

—Lu-Yen, Ancestor Lu, Records of The Source Teaching of the Pure Clarity of the Spiritual Jewel of the Exalted

Debbie is in her room, reading in an old journal to get more information to share with Laurel about her friend whom she wants to contact. Bob comes in and sits down. "Hi, dear, what are you studying so intently?"

"Oh, hi. It's my old journal from years ago. I wanted to refresh my memory about the gal I want Laurel to contact. My memory of things changes as time passes. The big event I remember clearly of course, but the little stuff—like the color of her hair and the sound of her voice—that seems to be far less clear, as if I'm looking at a fading photo in my brain. I thought rereading my own thoughts about the event might help me with the subtle stuff."

Debbie's voice trails off as she stares out the patio door at the mountains beyond the city. Bob begins changing after his qigong workout and gets ready to take a shower.

"Debbie, it is so odd that you even have the journal with you here. What made you even think to bring it to this seminar?"

"I know. It is weird! I was packing our books for the seminar, and this journal fell off the bookshelf. I hadn't seen it in years! I was going to put it right back, and then I remembered how it's important to keep a card as part of the reading with Tarot when it pops out while you are shuffling, so I packed it. I figured I would find out how it fit into the week once I was here. As soon as I heard about Laurel's gift, I knew it was here so I could talk with her about my friend. I love how synchronous life is, don't you? Jung was so right about the unseen threads of connections between us all."

Debbie closes the book and goes onto the patio. "Have a nice shower, dear," she says to Bob.

"OK, see you in the kitchen afterward. Oh, Debbie, do you know when the channeling is happening today?"

"No, but I think it's in the late afternoon, so you have a little time. I will go and check and let you know after your shower."

Debbie sits in a lotus position in her chair and closes her eyes. She begins to breathe lightly in and out and focuses a golden light at the top of her head, moving into her through her crown chakra and down her spine. As she breathes out, she releases tension out through her feet and hands. Continuing to breathe in this fashion, Debbie focuses on the image of her lost friend. The softness of her face and frail quality of her body seems to have the strongest imprint.

Remembering her notes in her journal, Debbie attempts to bring herself back to the last day she saw her friend and their last interaction. Her friend is begging her to help her die. It is painful to listen to her words again, to hear her voice; so painful. As she listens to her memory, going over every word and each movement of her friend's hands and face, Debbie's eyes well with tears. The sweetness of the request and the irrevocability of the task grab her heart at once. Debbie catches her image in the mirror next to her friend's bed, her face so young, lineless, and almost child-like...the decision to help her friend so many years ago has changed her forever. She sees herself taking the bottle of pills from her friend's hand and walking to the dresser to pour out the pills as her friend asked. Crushing them, she remembers the discussion about what to tell her friend's family members, whom Debbie did not know at all.

Her friend was so adamant about not leaving a note, not letting anyone know that she chose to end her life. She was so smart. She knew that it would not be seen as a suicide if she did not leave any evidence. She was unrelenting! The little energy she had rose to force a promise from Debbie that she would go and never return, and never share the truth with anyone—not even her friend's dear husband and daughter. She kept saying, "It's better this way."..."They will be OK."..."If they knew I chose this it would disrupt their movement forward in life. But they can deal more effectively with a loss that's out of their control." She was resolute. Looking into her eyes again in the meditation memory, Debbie sees her friend's determination.

Gently she hands her friend the crushed pills with a little milk and honey. Double her normal dose: just enough to stop her heart, and explainable with her advanced disease that she could forget and take her medicine twice. It was certain to be called an accident by the medical examiner and end the torture her friend was enduring. With her eyes smiling in love toward Debbie, her friend swallowed the medicine. She reached out her hand to hold Debbie's and squeezed it. "Thank you so much, my friend. Now you must go. They'll be back soon, and I don't want anyone to see you. I will send you a message from the other side to let you know I am OK. It's only my body leaving; my spirit will always be with you and everyone I love. God bless you...now go.'

Debbie watches herself kiss her friend's head. A single teardrop falls onto her face.

"I love you," she says.

Quietly Debbie slips out the back of the house, looking back once gently at her smiling friend. Debbie's memory stops there and fades into a fuzzy gray. In a different part of her mind, Debbie remembers that she leaves town immediately, just as her friend had requested. She returned to her studies in Santa Fe. Later, she saw that the newspapers reported her friend's death as an accident.

The fuzziness continues a bit in her memory. Debbie focuses her breathing on the golden light. This consolidates the energy and she sees an image of an owl feather. It reminds her of her friend's farewell, that she would send a message from the other side.

Just then Debbie jumps up, her eyes wide open. *She did send me a message. She sent me that owl feather. How could I have missed it? With all my reading, all my studies, all my training, how could I miss that the owl feather was from her?* Debbie realizes that she doesn't need to talk with Laurel about her friend; she has already answered her own questions. Smiling, with tears rolling down her face, Debbie goes back into her room and sits down to make a notation in her old journal. She writes, "owl feather." Then she wipes her eyes, shakes her hair, and goes out to the kitchen.

Peter, Rob, Sophia, and Sarabeth are sitting around the counter looking at Chinese lettering and talking about Confucianism. Sarabeth greets Debbie as she enters.

"Hi, Debbie! Wow, your energy is completely different, like you have had a weight lifted. What's up?"

Debbie smiles at Sarabeth. "Something I'll tell you about later. What are you four up to? It looks very sophisticated."

"It's about my dream. Remember the one I told you about the other day, Debbie?"

Sophia is almost sitting on the counter so that she can be right in the middle of the discussion regarding the possible meanings of the pages of writing that were stolen in her dream.

"See, these are the letters. Well, they look the most like the Chinese characters that I remember from my dream. And see this guy? I think he is the guy who was killed. And Peter knows the whole story, even without me telling him my dream. He studied it with his teacher in China. He thinks it is about Confucianism. And now we're trying to figure out how to ask the channel about the dream—or rather, about the writing that was stolen. It's very exciting. Do you want to help? You know a lot about Chinese history, right?"

"Actually, I do, but not like Peter and Jan. I know a lot about metaphor and archetypes and dreams and the collective unconscious. So, I do know about Confucianism from a different perspective. I think I might be able to help, though. If you consider that the dream came to you on the first day of the seminar and you apply synchronicity, then the dream is coming to enhance the seminar or as part of the seminar. That means that in some way, what was stolen will relate to what the channel has been discussing. Let's think about what we have learned so far."

"Oh, that's a good structure to work within to define the connection," Peter says. "Great work, Debbie." He pulls out a new piece of drawing paper that he had taken from Rob's studio.

"Well, that's what I've been saying all along," Sophia says.

"Yes, you have," both Rob and Sarabeth chime in.

"OK, good, so we all agree. Let's see what connections we can make using our intuition and our cognition."

Peter writes as he talks. "Energy, vitality, and spirit. Love is the most healing focus. Let the heart lead. Trust your emotional sensory guidance system, including intuition. Live the truth and offer the opportunity for others to shift without feeling responsible for their healing. OK, what else?"

"What about the anchoring of light energy through your heart chakra?" Sophia responds. "Oh, and that attention and intention focus creation. Oh, and to follow your emotion to discover what you are blocking or fear. And something about breathing increases your light energy, and not breathing or holding your breath is like not living." Sophia writes her ideas as she says them.

"Very good. OK, I really like the stuff about how shen disordered-ness skews energy and creates disease," Rob says. "I don't exactly understand how we shift our emotions, but the concept makes sense."

Peter adds this to the list of information.

"I know there is more, but let's look at this," Rob continues. He looks at Sarabeth. "Is there something here we can ask as part of the channeling tonight?"

"Well, of course. Why don't you bring these notes with you into the channeling and then ask whatever you feel at the time of the questioning. You can have faith that what needs to be asked, will be, and that what needs to be answered, will be. Remember spirit is bigger than our minds, even all of ours."

Sarabeth gently smiled and hugged Sophia.

"Let's get refreshed and go into the living room for the channeling. I think we're in the perfect space for it right now. Debbie, will you get Bob and Laurel? Thanks."

Sarabeth has placed all the water and foodstuffs out so that her friends will be supported during the channeling. At last, Laurel arrives. "Hi, honey. Can you take that seat, and we can all settle into this space for a beautiful channeling experience?"

Sarabeth begins her focusing mantra:

"Let's focus our intention on what we want to experience and receive from the channeling. Bring your attention into this space. Focus your energy right here, right now. To center yourself here, use your breath. Take a deep, cleansing breath and release all the day's activities as you exhale. Breathing in and breathing out. As you inhale, imagine golden light entering the top of your head. Allow it to move down through your body, along your spine, and then out your feet and hands. As you exhale, release any nagging negative energy, feeling, or physical symptom. Continue breathing in and breathing out. Imagine yourself fully and completely in this room. From within, set a loving intention for this channeling. Good! We are all vibrating at a much higher level. What a sweet connection."

Sarabeth puts a lozenge into her mouth and takes another deep, cleansing breath as she begins her inner-directing mantra, "OK, let's begin."

"*Source energy, allow me to be a clear healing channel. I call in one hundred thousand angels to please come in and fill this room; I invite in only high-frequency light beings. Please come in to guide me and offer me interpretation for this third evening of this retreat on healing psycho-emotional trauma through the ancient traditions... Thank you for your protection and guidance dear Archangel Michael, Mercury, The Council of Twelve, Orion, the Marys, and Sirius...* "

Sarabeth relaxes into her chair, feeling a deep abiding love overwhelming her. She feels the voice and words from the channel and begins to simply speak what is presented to her. Her voice softens as she speaks the words, in a seeing/hearing/knowing experience so that the content is immediately known to her as the words pour out of her.

"*Dearly beloved, we are here and we want you to know how much we love each of you. We are again filled with joy to assist you in bringing increased light into your vessels as you choose to have this experience. Intention and attention in a light, clarified way assists you to open further to your healing capacity so you may receive the historical traditions you desire. Through this process you discover more fully how all is energy and light.*

"*We are grateful for your ongoing focus and attention to the light and the ancient knowledge found within. Integration of spirit, mind, and body are necessary for healing and health. To increase your integration process, allow peace to enter your heart center, go into your heart center and open to love; from an open heart center, you are able to receive a higher frequency of light. Anchor this in your field through intention and connection to source; you may imagine this as a light that moves through your chakra system and anchors into your field. Think of this as if you are stepping into the light, and the light pours in through and around you.*

"*Remember that attention and intention focus energy and creation...You create that to which you put your attention. Pay attention to that which brings you joy, that which you desire, and this is what you will create. Pay attention to that which you fear or to that which is lacking, and you experience more of that fear and lacking. Movement between these two centers, between the two attentions, and you create a stagnation or spiral of movement back and forth.*

You choose your creation through your attention and intention and love. Living is love; not living is fear. Fear cannot exist where there is love. Come from your heart space and you will be in love, in the space of love, which allows for direct communication with spirit, compassion, and light. Consider how you respond to fear. You hold your breath. You actually stop breathing for that moment. That stop-ping, that not-living, creates a disruption, and this is the beginning of a spinoff of your energy that can create a distortion in time and in the body.

"You may use your internal sensory guidance system, your emotions, as a doorway for you to further understand and connect with the higher, lighter frequency. Integration of your spiritual, emotional, and physical bodies increases your capacity to hold the higher frequencies of light on the planet so that you may remain in connection with the way, with heart-centered guidance, and create healing and miraculous change.

"See yourself as spirit-human, through your sensing-emotional body you connect to your spiritual. And let your spiritual aspect guide you. Remain open to where the flow of your emotion brings you. Through this method of openness, you will connect to higher and higher frequencies of light. Imagine this flow like a river, complete with different levels and currents. Note that the currents of anger and frustration are at the superficial level. When you allow yourself to float under the anger or frustration you can get to the underlying emotional issue of lack, sadness, abandonment, or loss.

From this space, open your heart to allow in more light, a fuller experience of love, and you will see these deeper emotions transform. Follow this until you can get to a space of gratefulness and love; now you are anchoring very high light frequencies. From here you can create a full and complete healing.

"The energies of flow and allowing are key to increasing the frequency of light. Allowing each emotion its expression, with love and compassion, allows for it to be released and you to be guided to your true essential being. From this space you can see what is in your best interest, and out of a natural inner guidance, be guided by what brings you joy.

"The continuum of control and allowing is connected to creation and ownership in your soul purpose, your life path. Development of habitual dissonances in your behavior in order to avoid pain or in reaction to fear, is a skewing out away from your essential being and

*soul path. It is akin to holding your breath, blocking the flow in energy,
so that your self becomes bound and small. This energetic action can
cause a disruption in the flow like a bottleneck, backing up energy
in the meridian and light frequency system. The more this blockage
happens the less movement there is within the physical and mental
body. This is what creates all disease in your spirit, mind, and body.
All disease begins from the perspective of a spiritual disconnect within
a being. From there, it can develop into distorted thinking, which,
over time, distorts the energetic flow around you. This blocks the light
frequency available to you and creates a dulling of your senses and a
distortion of your perceptions and may lead to stagnation and visceral
dysfunction or physical disease.*

"As your light frequency drops and dulls, you move out of your
heart center. The lower chakras begin to define situations, which in
psychology are called the secondary drives. Sensefulness in this realm
is interpreted as fear-based, survivalistic, and dualistic, an experience
of needing to fight over limited resources. Decisions are made out of
fear, not love. Over time, the constant fear-based decision-making
leads to despair, a disconnection from source energy and joy, depres-
sion, a deep sense of lack and hopelessness. Your mind dulls, and your
visceral body decays at a more rapid state.

"This can be made worse through the use of alcohol and percep-
tion-distorting medications or mind-numbing drugs, as well as poor
energetic quality of food, water, and lack of exercise. Over time, like a
pipe that gets clogged from garbage buildup, the energetic pulsing gets
stagnant and clogged. As the electromagnetic field through which you
interpret your soul-plan gets clogged, it can't interpret the information without the connection to the light frequency, and light strands
in this field burn out. It is from this field that various forms of disconnections begin to be made tangible in the physical and cognitive fields.
This is the area where Sarabeth works when she is clearing the energetic field of her patients, clients, and friends.

"In the last channeling we discussed the importance of whole
foods, fresh water, moderate exercise, daily meditation, clean air, and
breath. And that both excess and insufficiency create dissonance in the

balance within, dull the capacity for light, and lead to disease within each person.

"Often you can use meditation in and with your natural surroundings to begin to lighten up your field. Simply going into your garden and sitting with trees, flowers, shrubs, insects, birds, the earth, and the sky can allow you to reconnect with the light frequency. You will experience receiving information from all of nature around you. This communication is completely heart centered. You will feel, know the information from within your heart center. Language is a human tool. Language interferes with the heart communication of the senses. We will discuss this further in a future time together. Just know there are many simple exercises you can use to reacquaint yourself with the healing power of nature. Mercury likes to talk about the importance of communication between all the living aspects of the planet to increase the light vibration on the planet. This is a powerful experience, to simply breathe as one interconnected within the tapestry of life.

"Today's interpretation is on the effects of shock and trauma to the spiritual, emotional, physical system that goes unabated or which is not worked through. This requires clearance and integration to be assimilated. Lack of this clearance and integration leads to disconnection within the physical, emotional, and spiritual well-being of a being.

"Healing of such trauma comes from the release of the original trauma, and a return to your soul purpose. A shift in focus of attention and intention, and a direct connection to your soul purpose through this retrieval of your soul increases your light frequency through returning the whole of the experience, the gestalt of it, that contains thoughts, feelings and spirit, mind, body lessons. This can be accomplished through guided meditation that incorporates opening to a feeling/seeing/knowing re-experience and reworking of the event, as well as specific acupuncture-assisted energetic release treatments. This can be enhanced through an intention based practice of meditation and yoga, and the penetrating focus of love. For some, the use of ancient, ceremonial plant medicines in sacred ceremonies are needed to break through the resistant misbeliefs. The use of crystal grids along specific five-element based acupuncture points can also bring about this type of release and soul retrieval when guided by the five spirits, and incorporating toning and guided journeying.

"Loving oneself fully and experiencing forgiveness heals. Begin with an intention to eliminate the stagnating and harmful patterns, and extinguishing the controlling patterns developed to assuage pain, fear, and anxiety. This will assist in the release of the trauma, a return to balance, an opening to love, and forgiveness. Remember that your perceptions create your reality. Focus on love and healing. Start your attention and intention from the position that you are an ultimate creator—and in some way, whatever is happening, you have a part in its creation. Identify how you may have been wronged but release the sense of victimhood and address what is the lesson for your soul growth, your soul path.

"Your thinking is connected to your being. This is your emotional and spiritual and physical being, and when you are distorted within this integration your thinking is distorted. This is an interactive system, each affects the other, you can heal your thinking through reclamation of healthful living, cleansing your physical actions and behaviors with a focus on intention and attention. Prayer and meditation assist you in this. You can heal you body through shifting your thinking, through meditation, belief clarification, prayer, self-love, and loving-kindness. Focus on experiencing through your heart center rather than a simple cognitive process. If you keep finding yourself in the same loop, like a groove worn in the mud, consider a way to shift your perception, like a handstand to your thinking. This will offer you a way to jump out of the groove and shift your path.

"The earliest of treatises in the Taoist practices regarding healing and consciousness addressed these injuries. Some of you follow information from the Su Wen and Ling Shu. The use of the extraordinary channels in your treatment of disease has shown you the immense power in these strategies. Other processes that help to release this patterning include the five-element system and the use of aligning with sound and light frequencies along the meridians and source points, jing well points and chakra system. As a number of you are aware, this helps to excite and re-infuse light into the fifth-dimensional axonal grid and fifth-dimensional blueprint.

"The tradition and practice of yoga utilizes these processes to create health, and this is a way to focus on self-love and to release unwanted, limiting beliefs and physical holding patterns so that you can focus on increasing the level of light you can hold within your physical body.

"We have been collaborating with Sarabeth to develop a way to incorporate the spiritual, physical, and emotional/cognitive field release through the use of specific acupuncture points, energy work, toning, healing sprays, crystal grids, and a clarifying whole-food diet. This is the developing tradition that Sarabeth has been coordinating with the five spirits over the last four years. This process is the most efficient way to release the trauma in all three energetic fields that surround your physical body, including the astral dimension so that you can access a higher light frequency and ascertain your soul purpose. All healing derives from this. It addresses the distortion in the fields at once, allowing a complete release and transformation of the trauma or skew, immediately. It looks like a miracle, and yet is simply the clarification and amplification of what is not and what is, so that the integrated being may uplevel to a higher degree of harmony and balance, let in more light, and activate higher light-dimensional living.

"This will be addressed in various ways over the next few offer-ings, unless something pulls us in a different direction. We are aware that you have questions, and we would like to answer these to your satisfaction. Several of us have spoken in this time, and many high light beings are ready to provide loving guidance and information for you. We want you to know how much we love you and how grateful we are to be your interpreters for this information.

"We are available for specific questions. Remember to drink plenty of water to assist your assimilation of this information at the cellular level as you are integrating this information and increasing the degree and frequency of light you are each holding; cleanse your energy field with lavender and sage as well as salt; and allow *yourselves plenty of rest to help with assimilation of this information. Allow yourself some grounding foods. You may use cleansing baths that incorporate baking soda and sea salt as well as hot oil treatments. You may be grounded through touch and walking on the earth in your bare feet. Salt on the balls of your feet will bring you into your physical bodies and ground you, and meanwhile anchor the light and new information.*

"We are so pleased to have this opportunity to share this information and love you very much...we await any questions you may have."

Sarabeth lightly speaks. "Thank you so much Archangel Gabriel, Mercury, the Council of Twelve, Orion, Metatron, the Marys, and Sirius. I am so grateful for this information. At this time I will open it up to questions. Please begin from my right."

"Can you discuss how Jung's work on the collective unconscious and the five-element theory can work in unison to assist healing?" Bob says.

"What a wonderful question, Bob. First, we want you to know that we feel you already know the answer to this question. We are aware of the many people you have helped through your attention to Jung's archetypes and healing focus on the similarities in the fabric of human consciousness. The five-element system allows for the idea of nature and the heavens to be activated, to create a sense of balance and harmony. This is positively affected by the use of the opening points of the extraordinary channels and the appropriate ghost points, especially those in the neck and wrist.

Using the archetypes that are connected to the five elements of wood, fire, earth, metal, and water will have the highest degree of success when integrating these two theories. We feel that you have a sense of this intuitively, and we encourage you to develop along the path you have started. We see that in the coming years, you will produce a treatise that fully identifies these points and archetypal images. As you understand, the state in which ego and non-ego are no longer in opposition with each other is the pivot point of the Tao. Limitations, separation are not part of the Tao. The collective unconscious offers a way in to understand how and in what ways the individual is caught in ego and no-ego opposition.

The five spirits flow to allow a reconnection to the Tao, which offers a way to jump out of the third-dimensional blueprint of duality and realign the axonal meridian system so that the individual allows for his communion with the soul and the experience of Tao. Again, we encourage you to continue on the path you have undertaken, and this will come to fruition in two to six months as you develop a working draft. From there, you will create small pockets of training groups to clarify how to best communicate this information to other practitioners.

The key that you are looking for is the focus point. We know you have tried to connect this via the source points, but we suggest you look at the jing river point, the ghost points, and the Bao mai. We encourage you to talk with Sarabeth about this, as she has already developed a set of strategies connected to various five-element shen disorders or psycho-emotional problems that respond directly to these points. She began this while in her Chinese medicine studies and has a full text on this. Once you apply her work to what you have created, you will have a full treatise that you may begin to use and to teach. We want you to know how grateful we are to you for how intently you follow your personal practice, and the commitment you have made to increasing the level of light on the planet. Does this sufficiently answer your question, Bob?"

"Oh yes, thank you very much. Lots to think about here. Fantastic. I appreciate the connection to these early treatises regarding the Tao."

Sophia quickly begins, "Mom, please can I ask about my dream?"

"Yes, honey, go ahead." Sarabeth opens her eyes and sweetly smiles at Sophia. She reaches for a lozenge and closes her eyes again as she puts it in her mouth.

"OK." Sophia begins in her most urgent yet respectful voice. "I'm wondering if you can explain to me why I had the dream about Liu Ruyi's death, and also if you can share about the writing that was stolen in my dream."

"*Dear, sweet Sophia, it is always a pleasure to communicate with you. Your spirit is such a delight for us, and you are such a bright light on the planet. We send you so much love and light. There is another here who wants to talk with you. Will you wait as Sarabeth shifts her energy to interpret his energy?*"

"Yes, of course, but it's not going to hurt Mom, right?"

"*No, this is just a much higher energy, and so the channel needs to go in much deeper...*"

"*Hello, I am Liu Ruyi. I am here to talk with Sophia. You have within you a spark of my family, and so you were given the dream to begin your search about your heritage. Your spark carries the full information about the writing that was stolen. This information is necessary for the upleveling of the consciousness on the planet. It is about light, love, and oneness. My father loved Confucianism, and I too feel the importance of knowing the right timing for all things. However, you carry within you the ability to create miracles instantaneously. It is through your genuine, personal living in the intuitive and sensing world, together connected by the light of spirit that you are able to do this. When you are at play and not thinking, you create. As soon as you let your mind lead, you lose the higher frequency and drop to the third and fourth dimensions and the level of humanity now. You have incarnated now because the planet is upleveling into the fifth and sixth dimension now and your soul path is to assist in this elevation and transition.*

"*The dream was a seed for you to begin to move into the perfection of living in your spirit-guided, intuitive-sensing self. From there you rise into fifth, sixth, and seventh dimensions of light, where creation is instantaneous. Through your continuous attention there you will be a perfect model to everyone around you, and you will increase the vibration of the planet so like beings will vibrate at your level. This is all for now. There is more. Be with this and allow the flow of it to guide you. Thank you for coming. I have been waiting for you for a very long time, although, as you know, time is not linear, so you and I are currently working together to bring this forward both in what you call the past and now. We will speak in your dreams and here again soon."*

Sarabeth's voice changes to a light, loving voice.

"Be at peace, Sophia. This is a huge responsibility, but it is also a gift of adventure. Know that you are supported by those close to you on the planet and in this realm. Although you are a leader, you are not alone. So much love to you, dear."

Sarabeth gently wipes tears from her eyes. "Thank you, all high light beings, for your support and your information today. Each of you is of great benefit. Thank you all. Thank you, Liu Ruyi. Archangel Michael, if you could clear the energy, thank you, thank you. Kadosh, kadosh, kadosh. Om mani padme hum. Gate, gate, paragate, parasamgate, Bohdi, Svaha!"

"OK, everyone, how are you doing? Sophia, come over here with me. We were at a very high light frequency."

Sarabeth drinks some water and takes a bite of chocolate.

"To overcome the dizziness, please drink your water and get grounded." Sophia rubs the ball of her left foot and cuddles into Sarabeth.

Peter, Jan, and Laurel are all writing. Rob and Debbie appear to be quietly meditating. Bob looks stunned. "Well, I have to say that was very surprising, very surprising! Sarabeth, I would like to talk with you later, obviously. I don't think I really understand how you have been living in this world with all of this for so long. It's powerful, exciting, draining, and well, challenging, isn't it?"

Sarabeth smiles at her dear friend.

"It has been a journey. I'm glad I haven't had to make it alone."

Sarabeth smiles at Rob from across the room while she cuddles with Sophia.

Peter chimes in. "To hear the words of a person whom I studied so closely is completely astonishing."

Sarabeth lovingly looks at her friend.

"Tonight, I really want you all to do the apple cider vinegar baths with the sea salt and baking soda. Or a shower with these if you prefer. Be gentle with yourselves." She looks at Rob. "Honey, do you think the food is here? Do you mind checking the back door? Thanks."

CHAPTER 7

The five spirits, the Wu Shen, are the resident deities of the Taoist psyche. These are our guides to the radiant landscape of the soul, the landscape that lies beyond the ordinary. During our lives they reside in the organs of the body. At death they return to the divine realms of above and below.

Shen, thought/consciousness, fire, heart, ren15. Hun, vision/imagination, wood, liver, Lr14. Yi, ideation/intention, earth, spleen, gb24. Po, emotion/instinct, metal, lung, Lu1. Zhi, will/wisdom, water, kidney, gb25.

When the spirits are disturbed our lives lack inspiration, direction, intention, embodied knowing, and instinctual potency. Our actions lack authenticity, spontaneity, and authority. We are stuck and cannot move forward in the manifestation of our Tao.

The five spirits must be related to and cultivated...Most often it is the person's life, the atmosphere and actions that tell us about the condition of the spirits...The Taoists, the five spirits, are bits of heavenly light that drop down into matter and take some weight and form... Subtle body neither pure spirit nor pure matter...Subtle breath body...A mythical expression of the undulating spinal column that extends from the earthbound tailbone to the heaven-bound crown...The tiny deities of the dragon that lives in our soul with its turquoise fish tail swimming in the oceans of the instinctual body and its fiery crimson head facing upward toward the regions of mind and spirit...the five spirits form a spinning axis of light that permeates and illuminates our being.

—Lorie Eve Dechar, Five Spirits

Jan and Peter quietly close the front door. It is 4 a.m., Lung time on the horary clock, the perfect time for meditation, as it is the beginning of the new energy flow cycle.

Jan speaks in a whisper.

"Wasn't that amazing to hear about Sophia's dream and how it has connected her to this earlier time period? I love the way in which she has been brought into the conference as a real participant. She is such a star-seed in her understanding of light and energy."

"What do you think Liu Ruyi meant when he said Sophia carried an aspect of his energy?" Peter asks, as he arranges his mat so that he can sit facing east as the sun rises over the mountain. "Sarabeth and Rob don't have Chinese heritage, from what I know. She is Greek and somewhere in East Asia, and he is English or Scottish, I think. Where would Sophia have gotten the Chinese heritage?"

Jan stretches her arms forward to lengthen her spine as she talks.

"Well, maybe we don't understand how the whole karma or soul connection works. Maybe we only understand the physical DNA heritage. This may indicate there is also a soul/spirit or karmic heritage that isn't connected to the physical heritage. I remember Sarabeth saying that Sophia was a star-seed from a very far off set of stars; she called it the Rainbow Constellation. I've never heard of that before, but maybe there is some sort of heritage based on star constellation parentage."

Peter reaches behind in a twist to open his spine.

"If that's true, then maybe Liu Ruyi also came from that same star constellation? That would explain how she would have the knowledge to create a book like the one he wrote, without having any training in the area or history with the specific philosophies of his time." He jolts up and looks at Jan. "It supports the Taoist belief that the Chinese civilization was a result of the spirit translation through meditation to high-frequency beings: 'handed down from divine heavenly source,' rather than the meditation deriving from the heightened civilization. It's like they knew about this star or soul heritage. Amazing!"

Jan smiles at Peter, touching his cheek sweetly.

"OK , let's meditate, Peter." Jan returns her focus to her mat, positions herself into a half lotus and begins breathing deeply.

Peter realigns his back to face toward the east and the gentle light, outlining the mountains.

Debbie is reaching toward a doorknob; she is walking down a set of stairs and then a long hall. She continues to go through door after door; she is getting nervous about the hallways and doors. Crying out for help, she sees a light at the end of the hall, a door slightly ajar. Debbie enters the room. In the corner she sees a bed with a young woman lying there. She sees a light on, and the woman is reading a book. As she steps closer, she sees it is her old friend who died many years before. She is smiling. "Come in, Deb, it's OK. Come in. I've been reading about your work. It's amazing, everything you have been doing since your studies in Santa Fe." Debbie notices her name is on the cover of the book, and then she sees other books, with other names on the covers.

"This is how I can see how my loved ones are doing, Deb. Each book is their book of life."

Her friend is holding one of the books very close to her. She is slightly hiding the name on the book; Debbie can make out the letter "S" and what looks like a "U," but nothing else.

"This one is very dear to me; she is struggling. I didn't expect it to be such a hardship for her. I thought her father would be able to help her more, but she has a stubborn streak—well, perseverance. And she has such good intuition she can tell when things aren't right. I didn't think of that, Debbie, I didn't think of that. Maybe because it hadn't shown up yet when I was with her. It developed after I had gone. I think it was one of the gifts of my leaving. Anyway, Debbie, I need you to help her. Help her to understand, to let go, and move on. She is stuck and I think it is making her sick. I can't go to her. I need her to

understand from a grounded, human place. I need you to help me one more time. Will you help me and help my dear one?"

Debbie watches herself go toward her friend and hug her. She watches herself say "yes." She watches herself take the book from her friend.

Just as she is turning over the book to see the name on it she wakes up. She has tossed off all her covers. Bob is soundly sleeping next to her. Debbie carefully grabs her glasses, slippers, pen, and journal and goes onto the patio to document the dream. She writes: *The strongest energy in the dream are the books, especially the one I took from my friend...Why can't she go to her daughter and help her directly?...Why is the name hidden from me? I think the book she gave me is her daughter, what is her name—it looked like "Su... " but I don't remember her daughter's name...Hallways, darkness, and many doors represent a journey deep into my unconscious, so somehow I know the answers to these questions. Oh, and, of course, that I have accessed different realms.* Debbie continues to work on her dream as the sun rises. Smiling at the sunlight, she feels refreshed with a sense of what to do next.

Laurel is tossing in her bed.

A very small child is walking down the hall of her home to her mother and dad's room. Sitting on the bed is her father. She looks at him; he is distraught, holding a pill bottle in his hand, shaking his head, saying over and over, "How did this happen, how did this happen?" With a sweet, calm smile on her face the little girl looks over to her mother, who's limp on the bed.

The child goes to her mother and touches her arm. "Mommy, are you... ?" She pauses; her mother's arm is ice cold. "Mommy?"

"Daddy, what's wrong with Mommy?"

"She's gone, honey."

"No, Daddy, no! How could this happen? I need her to stay with me."

"I know, honey, I want her with us too; I know how hard this is for you. Don't worry, you aren't alone. I will be there for you twice as

*much now that you don't have Mom, and we will keep her memory
alive with love; come here, honey, let me hold you." "Daddy, it's not
fair, it's not fair. I want my mommy."*

*The little girl crumbles in her father's arms, crying in big heaves...
then little sobs...she falls asleep with her father holding her.*

Suddenly Laurel awakens, her pillow soaked with tears,
the smell of her mother still in her memory. "I still miss
you, Mom." She looks at the clock; 4 a.m. Laurel pulls out
the corkboard. She sits staring at the connections, trying to
solve the equation of how her mother died, talking out loud
to herself.

"The medicine bottle is the key. I remember Dad
holding it and shaking his head. What was wrong? I have to
figure out how to ask the channel the question. It's something about Debbie, especially after the dig encounter. She
has some weird connection to me, but what is it?"

Holding her picture of her mom, Laurel lays her head
back down on the pillow and gently falls asleep cradling the
picture.

*Bob is sitting on a rock beside a stream. Across from him is a bearded
man with a suit and glasses. He has a sweet, endearing smile—almost
a smirk on his face as he puffs on his pipe. Bob sees many pages of
notes with symbols and Chinese characters on them. The bearded man
is making notes on these pages and returning them to Bob. This goes
on for a long time without any discussion or talking. There is a strong
urgency in Bob's gestures; he wants to get as much assistance as he can
before the bearded man leaves. The bearded man is starting to become
fuzzy, almost transparent. Bob notices that he is indeed disappearing,
until all that is left is the smirk on his face.*

*Bob turns his head slightly to the right and says, "How odd, just
like the Cheshire Cat. All that is left is his smile." And then that disappears too.*

"I have to remember that when I wake up—the Cheshire Cat
smile—it's a clue from my unconscious."

Gathering the notes, with their scribblings from the bearded man, Bob walks away from the stream toward the mountain. Then he stops and places all of the pages down in order in front of him. Imagining that he is holding a camera, he clicks visual imprints of the pages—especially the notes from Jung.

"I have to hold onto this in my consciousness before I awake."

Click. Click. Click. Click.

"Good—now I can awake and decipher my treasure."

Gently opening his eyes, Bob sees his lovely wife sitting on the patio, writing. *Oh, you too have had a dream, good!* he thinks to himself. Quickly, Bob takes his dream journal, pen, and flashlight and writes all that he can remember. Adding drawings and questions rapidly, he lightly closes the journal and returns to sleep.

Sophia is watching Liu Ruyi from an alcove just outside his room. It is dark and the smell of jasmine tea lingers in the air. On his desk are many pages of writings. Sophia can see some of the pages and recognizes the words. Liu Ruyi is drinking tea and discussing the importance of energy and light with an older man whom Sophia doesn't recognize. Sophia longs to go closer to the men but is afraid of being seen. From the alcove she reads the top pages on Liu Ruyi's writing table: "Energy alchemy formula."

The older man is talking about a serious matter. His voice has dropped almost to a whisper. He is speaking in a dialect of Chinese, but the words are changing in Sophia's mind—she is translating.

"You must be careful," he says. "She is set on taking your life. She sees you as an impediment to her son's transition to emperor. It is serious! You must give your manuscript to someone you trust so that the information won't be lost. She plans to destroy it, and you. She has a great deal of power among the advisers."

Sophia watches as Liu Ruyi sips his tea. He does not appear to be upset by the conversation. Sophia feels a deep love and pride toward Liu Ruyi rising within her being. Now, Liu Ruyi is talking; he too speaks in a Chinese dialect that is completely understandable to Sophia as she watches.

"I must do my work. If she must destroy me, then she must; I cannot hide or be something I am not. I can only do my work and create this important document for the good of all. If she takes it, there will be another who comes and brings forth the information."

Liu Ruyi pauses and looks toward the alcove with an almost imperceptible nod toward Sophia, then he continues.

"It is not my knowledge; I am only an interpreter of the information to bring it forth. If the time continuum shifts and this is not the time, another will come. I know this. You must allow the energies to flow with the guidance of the people. We cannot go against the flow of things. We cannot go against the Tao. It is. We are a part of it, not the directors of it."

Liu Ruyi sips his tea and looks directly at the old man.

"You are my benefactor and my friend, and I am deeply grateful to you for your friendship. If the time comes and I am killed, do not grieve my loss. Celebrate our time together and our deep understanding of each other and our work. Be at peace regardless of the outcome. All is as it should be."

He hands his friend some tea and nods lightly at him.

Sophia awakens, still smelling the tea and the dampness of the room. She is struggling with the information, thinking to herself, *How could he know that he was an interpreter? He was so clear about his role and his place in history.* Sophia feels a deep strength within her growing, as well as a loving appreciation for her new friend, Liu Ruyi. She lightly jumps out of her bed and walks down the hall to her father's studio. As she passes her parent's room she hears Leo crying in his sleep. She stops at the doorway and pets him. He opens his eyes, paws at her hand on his nose, and then returns to sleep. Sophia goes into her father's studio. Picking up her journal and special paints, she begins to document her dream.

Sarabeth is walking in a large labyrinth. It is green all around her, and the smell of citrus fills her. She feels slightly anxious as she follows the path, listening to the birds and the rustling of the leaves. In the background the cawing of crows makes her smile at their playfulness. She feels the urgency of completing her test. She sees her feet in light sandals, with white fabric flowing around her ankles. She is hurrying to complete the labyrinth without getting lost in the interior dead ends. Facing a tall wall of green, she closes her eyes and meditates, lightly asking her inner guide which way to go. She feels a gentle pull of energy to her left and turns in that direction. Within moments, the space opens up, and she sees Lance standing in the center staring at the family lemon tree, which is bursting with fruit.

The garden is moving away. Sarabeth is lightly floating in space. Stars spin by. She gently slows at different constellations to view as if they are familiar friends. The stars stop moving; she floats down to a space of white rocks in the shape of a labyrinth with one path to the center. Waves of water crash about her. Sarabeth moves through the labyrinth as if flying, floating 18 inches off the ground. The scent of olive trees infuse her. She floats down to the center, a stone slab with a group of white flowers and shells set atop it. She is home and he is there. Sarabeth again sees a white cloth around her ankles, this time with a gold trim and flat sandals that tie around her ankles. Next to the shells is a filled ceramic wine goblet. Sarabeth greets Lance with a kiss, takes a drink from the glass, and speaks a prayer in Ancient Greek.

The white stones are moving away. Sarabeth is lightly floating in space, stars spinning by. The stars stop moving. She floats down to a mound of brown rocks on brown dirt placed in the shape of a labyrinth with a single path to the center. Flutes and drums play in the background as she dances in moccasins through the labyrinth. At the center, feathers and corn rest on a low, brown mound of dirt. The smell of burning sage and cedar rises from branches stuck into the sand. It fills her with a sense of peace. From behind the mound Sarabeth sees another dancer, a man. Returning the cedar branch to the mound, Sarabeth sets out after him. Just as she meets up with him and he turns his face toward her, she wakes up.

Standing next to her bed is Rob.

"Good morning, honey. It's a beautiful day. Let's do a quick drawing on the deck."

"Coffee! Thank you. How did you sleep?"

Sarabeth drinks the coffee with deep attention.

"Oh, this is a good latte! OK, I'm game for some drawing. I'll get my book. I had a very intense dream—well, set of dreams, really. I'm interested in how they go together and what the message is from my unconscious."

"I slept well. I don't remember any dreams though, just restful sleep. Tell me about your dream."

"I seemed to be traveling in time, but in each of my destinations I was doing the same thing."

Sarabeth is gathering her sandals to go out onto the deck, with her small drawing book under her arm and coffee in her other hand. Settling her feet into her shoes, she hops as she walks out

"I was moving through a labyrinth in each of the vignettes. It was me, but I was different in each. The first time period was Celtic. It was so green and very fragrant. I felt anxious, like I was taking a test to get through the maze. The next one was Greek, probably Crete because there were waves crashing near the labyrinth. It was so white. And the third time it was Native American, probably Pueblo. In this third time the labyrinth was made of stone. My mode of transportation was floating through space and flying. It was awesome—really out of this world.

"The first labyrinth was a maze of bushes. The second was white stone, and the third was brown rock. All three had different shapes, but each was a true labyrinth with one way to the middle, so a type of centering path. It seemed to be showing me different time continuums where I was stepping into some kind of power. Lance was there in each one."

Rob pauses, glances at Sarabeth, and then returns to his drawing. "Well, it sounds extraordinary. I'm fascinated by the different time periods but doing the same thing. There's something important about the maze or labyrinth and the connection between the three time periods. Have you spoken to Lance?"

"I did, recently. In one of my meditations, I was guided to invite him to part of the retreat. He said he would come toward the end." Sarabeth touches Rob's arm. "Are you OK with him coming here?"

Rob looks up at Sarabeth's face.

"I don't like that he will be here. It brings up so many emotions inside me, but this is your work and I want to support you. How are your feelings toward him now? Are you still in love with him?"

Sarabeth's eyes dart away.

"I don't know how I feel. I know I am deeply connected to him. It feels like a dream. I'm going to do a quick drawing to keep the images strong and then write it all down. Maybe I can discern the messages from spirit, and from my unconscious. Maybe that will help me clarify my feelings about Lance too. I know the labyrinth has to do with me finding my center and living authentically on my path. Seeing him in each timeline is a clue. Maybe I've had many lifetimes as a guide in this transformation onto your path thing, and this life is some kind of completion energy. I have seen us working together many times. It stopped coming through my meditations, when I decided to stay with you when you were sick. Recently, as I was developing this program, those images returned. I don't know what it means yet."

Sarabeth looks over at Rob again.

"I'm sorry. This is so difficult. It's like you and I are so connected, and he and I are so connected. I get jumbled inside."

Rob's eyes fill with tears.

"I don't want to go through what we did before. I thought we were beyond that time. I'm not sure I can handle seeing him here with you and Sophia. She loves him so much, but she doesn't know who you two were to each other. She thinks of him as her personal friend. It's so hard for me to contain my emotion around this, Sara."

Rob puts down his pencil.

Sarabeth hugs Rob. "I made a choice. I stayed. Maybe the dream is just information about this retreat, not about Lance at all. One thought I had is that there is a very feminine quality to each of these lifetimes. Maybe that's the really important component—living in more of the feminine consciousness. You know, in thinking about it, I remember from my college studies that the word 'labyrinth' comes from ancient Crete and derives from *labrys*, the two-headed ax, which symbolized the moon goddess. The labyrinth signified the uterus of the goddess, which the initiate entered to emerge reborn. The spiral and the labyrinth appear around the world in carvings and paintings dedicated to the mother. I think my unconscious is getting me to focus on the power of the feminine. It felt so different in the Celtic time period, like I was taking a test. I'm going to work with it and see what I get."

Rob looks back at his drawing.

"OK. I think I'm going to spend some time here, then do yoga. Let's talk later. I'm glad you told me the truth so I can prepare for him to be here."

Sarabeth leans in and looks at Rob's face. "Let's just take it one step at a time. I love you."

Rob holds Sarabeth close. "I know you do. And I'm grateful for you in my life. I can feel it though you still love him, too." He gently kisses her and returns his attention to his drawing. "I need some time to work through this. It is a lot to take in, Sara."

Sarabeth's mind is spinning. She thinks to herself, *How can this be happening again? Now, with so much on the line? What are the angels trying to show me?* Sarabeth hears Sophia calling her. "OK, I'm going to see what Sophia needs, then go for a run. Let's talk later, before the channeling."

CHAPTER 8

What I notice as I observe...is the Tao of emulating heaven and earth...if people can be open-minded and magnanimous, be receptive to all...give without seeking reward... realize all are one, then people can be companions of heaven.

If people can be flexible and yielding, humble, practice self-control...ignoring insult without anxiety or resentment when faced with danger or adversity, then people can be companions of earth.

With the nobility of heaven and the humility of earth, one joins in with the attributes of heaven and earth and extends to eternity with them.

What I realize as I observe is the Tao of separation and joining of yin and yang. The yang energy in people is firm; firmness without restraint turns to aggressiveness, like fire rising.

Yin energy is flexible; flexibility without support becomes too weak, like water descending.

When firmness and flexibility do not balance each other, solitary yin cannot give life, isolated yang cannot foster growth—so living energy ceases.

If one is firm without being aggressive, using firmness with flexibility, that is like fire being below. If one is flexible without being weak, supporting flexibility with firmness, that is like water being above.

When firmness and flexibility are balanced, yin and yang are in harmony; essence and sense merge, water and fire offset each other.

—Liu I-Ming, Awakening to the Tao

Sarabeth keeps being drawn back to the dream as she gets into a rhythm in her pace, running. She loves running with Leo. It's meditative. The rhythmic nature of the running keeps bringing her back to the feeling of floating just above the stones in the second labyrinth.

What can the message be from my unconscious? she wonders to herself as she runs. *Is it about trust and flow? The various spirits are preparing us for a shift in how we see the energy of the planet. First, giving us information about how creation happens and how to stay away from the negative energy. The focus must be ultimately on how to shift the consciousness of the whole planet, not just for those of us sitting in the room. But why is that important now? What is happening that we are in need of a powerful transformation of energy, such a leap of light-consciousness? It has to be about the need for the salvation of the planet to acknowledge the connectedness of life and create, as one, a positive change.*

The labyrinth is the key. The feminine energy, feminine consciousness, is the change. The labyrinth focuses the individual onto her path. It is individual, but a central part of many cultures. And in each instance in the dream it was me, as female—so confirmation of a need to reinterpret human consciousness with more yin in the picture, more goddess feminine energy. But Lance was there too: in the center, in each one. Is that about my soul life choices or just an image of that masculine energy in balance with the feminine? I don't understand why they are showing him to me. I know there are timelines and soul choices. Is he coming back into my life? Are they trying to show me that is my soul-plan? How do I explain this to Rob or Sophia? It's so difficult to live in two dimensions at once, fifth and third. In third dimension my relationship with Lance is a tragedy. In fifth dimension it's completely natural, like breathing.

Immediately Sarabeth is struck by the image of when they were first together, literally surrounded by star constellations, and how being with him was like dancing in the stars, completely out of her third-dimensional body in another dimension of consciousness. She wonders to herself, *What is this relationship to the star constellations? Are these helpers—interpreters to this transition? I'm going to have to invite*

more assistance from the Arcturian, the Pleiadian star-seed channels,
Sirius, and Orion on this. I need more guidance.

As Sarabeth finishes her thoughts, she notices she is in front of a huge meditation wheel. She stops. She forgot this wheel was on the grounds of Sophia's school. Leo pulls at her arm.

"OK, boy, just a minute."

Sarabeth walks to the center of the wheel. She looks at the small stones and notes that have been left by others. She begins in the east and meditates about her dream. She asks for Archangel Raphael to offer her the healing energy to act in alliance with the dream messages. She moves to the south position of the wheel and asks for her heart to open, then calls on Archangel Michael to offer strength to understand the message of the dream. Then, moving clockwise, she moves to the west and asks for Archangel Gabriel to remove obstacles to seeing the truth about her dream. Finally, she stops at the north and waits to receive some wisdom from Archangel Uriel and Archangel Ariel about the overall meaning of the dream and its connection to the cosmos. Leo lies down in the palette of rocks and crystals strewn about the north spoke of the meditation wheel.

Sarabeth lightly releases the need to know the answer and waits for a revelation. Then, after a few moments, she notices an owl out of the corner of her eye, popping out of a burrow to look at her. Burrowing owl: grounded wisdom. Then she hears the sound of a hawk in the sky flying overhead: heightened wisdom, messages from spirit. She embraces the relationship between these creatures, wisdom and clairvoyance, trusting what is unseen but known and the power of the heavens, source energy. Grasping the powerful connection between the creature of yin living in the earth with knowledge of the heavens and the soaring creature of yang and the heavens connecting to earth, she understands the energy of the universe in that moment. Sarabeth bows to both creatures, the wisdom of the wheel, and the gentle, knowing patience of Leo.

Looking down she sees a feather stuck between where she is standing and where Leo sits. It is an owl feather. She picks it up and puts it in her jacket, grateful for the reminder of the moment. She and Leo run home.

Rob, Peter, and Bob are hiking among petroglyphs just outside of the retreat. Bob is fascinated by the different stories that are held within the pictures on the rocks. He sees the pictures as a powerful example of Jung's work on the collective unconscious and how all humans are connected through the archetypes that drive human behavior. He stops and views the pictures, then takes out a book to copy down the image to bring back with him to the house for review and analysis with symbols he has collected elsewhere.

Rob and Peter are gently walking with Bob.

"Perhaps if we stay here, we can feel what it was like for our counterparts in this time," Peter says to Rob.

"I know. It's really powerful. I sometimes have to remind myself to breathe as I look at the images. The coolness of the stone is so refreshing, too. It does feel out of this world. I think it's because they chose to use the lava rock. The components of the rock are so different and come from so deep within the earth it feels like that is part of the message: In some way connected to the deep feminine of the earth and the powerful masculine of the sky since they are out in the sunlight, not hidden in caves."

Rob holds his hand against the stone to feel the energy of the picture.

Peter looks at Bob. "So, this culture, was it connected to the Chinese culture? Because it seems they are looking at the yin-and-yang connection of earth and heaven in similar ways."

Bob responds without looking up from his drawing.

"There are stories that the people who inhabited this land before it became America walked across the thin plane of earth before it was changed by the ice age. They would have been connected to those who developed the information known as Taoist. But Jung's concept is that the information is part of a deeper collective unconscious that's shared among all cultures. The stories of the Native Americans are similar but not wholly consistent with Taoist philosophy. The collective unconscious archetypes must be how the individuals who are channeling through Sarabeth intend to help us all come together in a larger peace, as one world."

Rob interrupts. "You know, Sarabeth says that Taoism perceives that the originators of civilization itself are people of higher knowledge that was attained via extra-dimensional awareness. Wouldn't that mean that each of these powerful civilizations could connect with source and receive that information? I think this is the repeated cultural philosophy of *a priori* and *a posteriori*. What *is*...that is the collective unconscious of Jung?"

"Yes, that is the Taoist belief. And you see it represented in Buddhism and Hinduism and the Vedics—that the enlightened adapt to worldly conditions in order to liberate people; the enlightened provoke deep faith by being in the world yet unaffected by it, just as the lotus grows out of the mud yet is unaffected by it and presents as pure beauty."

"So, Sarabeth had this amazing dream last night about being in three different space-time continuums where she was basically doing the same thing in each dimension: walking through a labyrinth. I think it's related to what we are talking about here: some sort of transmission of being in the light, centered and transmitted through the archetype of the journey to the center of the self, or soul. She thinks it has something to do with the loss of connection to the divine feminine: how the energies of separation of the divine, elevating the masculine aspect while flattening the feminine aspect is part of the way the consciousness has been stuck in third and fourth dimension. What do you guys think?"

Rob is excited about the synchronous nature of the events. In the back of his mind, he pushes away the thought of Lance coming. Bob looks up from his drawing.

"Wow, very cool. I had a dream last night where I was showing all these symbols to Jung. It was a completely silent dream. All of the communication was through symbol. He wrote notes on pages in my journal but didn't speak at all. Then he disappeared except for a smile—I mean literally disappeared, just like the Cheshire Cat in *Alice in Wonderland*! I still have to look into what my subconscious was connecting for me there. Anyway, it was very powerful. I think it directly connects to Sarabeth's dream and living in the light of upleveled consciousness."

"Oh Bob, there's this great dialogue between Alice and the Cheshire Cat in *Alice In Wonderland* that you must be connecting to in your subconscious. She's asking for help to find her way and the Cat is being enigmatic, saying, 'It depends on where you want to go,' and Alice is noncommittal, saying how 'it doesn't matter.' The Cat retorts, 'Then it doesn't matter which way you go.' It's so beautifully existential; if you don't know where you're going, there's no way to get there. I think this is the stuff the channeling has been trying to tell us—we create the path through our attention and intention."

Bob looks at Rob and stops what he is doing.

"How did you know that? I think that's exactly what the image was trying to show me."

Rob smiles a Cheshire grin.

"I don't know. It just came to me. I loved that story."

Peter rubs his hand over the carvings on the stone.

"The energy of this place reminds me of the dig at your house, Rob. It's almost as if they are interconnected in time.

I like the way the Native American energy and stories are connected to the Taoist beliefs. It makes me feel there is a tapestry of life."

Bob is finishing his drawings and breathing deeply.

"It was the thing that so fascinated Jung: the collective unconscious archetypes and the shared memories or stories that bind human groups together. You know, I feel that at times I can communicate with the stone, the earth, the trees, and the animals. And when I do, it brings me such a deep level of peace. Indescribable."

"That's the basis of Sarabeth's recent work in eco-psychology. She believes that the ancient texts taught us to be one with nature in order to recognize that nature and human are one shared body. She says it's difficult to describe because language separates us from the rest of nature, and so we can only experience it with our sensefulness without language diminishing it."

Bob looks at Rob again with an astonished face. "That's what Jung said about the Taoists' belief. Let me think, something about how limitations were not originally part of the meaning of life. Words had no fixed meanings. He talked about how language separated into affirmation and negations and attachments that pulled one away from the Tao. And outward hearing should not penetrate further than the ear; the intellect should not seek to lead a separate existence as it affects the soul from absorbing the whole world. I don't think I fully understood this until after hearing these channelings. That was from his book *Synchronicity*, and this is all so synchronous. Fascinating."

Rob is holding a rock in his hand, rolling it over in his palm as he describes Sarabeth's findings.

"She believes we can access the tapestry of life instinctively through our senses if we just allow ourselves to be open and pay attention to them. It's like an internal sensory guidance system to make decisions and actions in the world.

Peter, have you or Jan ever felt that you could communicate with nature in that way?"

Peter cocks his head as he looks at Rob and Bob.

"I'm not sure I can say I communicate with rocks and trees. But when I'm in nature I definitely feel the same energy I feel in the points along the meridian and in the pulses of my clients. Being in nature, in the elements, offers me a sense of calm that I am deeply attracted to experiencing. That's why I prefer to meditate outside in a garden or with nature of any kind. I feel I can connect to spirit more easily in that environment. Sometimes, if I'm away from nature I start to feel depressed, as if I get healing energy from being in nature."

"Oh no. I forgot we're supposed to be back for another channeling. I think we have to leave this beautiful place right now. Are you two ready?"

Rob is grabbing his materials and water as he is talking. Bob is replacing his drawing materials.

"I'm ready, Rob. Let's go."

Both men start walking away. Peter looks back longingly as he joins his friends on the short hike back to the car and Rob's house.

Sarabeth places the owl feather near her on the white, embroidered couch. She hears her friends entering the front door.

"Rob, will you bring everyone in as soon as possible? I want to begin the channeling as the sun is setting. There's something about this time that's important."

Rob peeks in and nods his head. "Yes, we're back. We passed Laurel and Debbie on the way in, and Peter is getting Jan. Is Sophia upstairs?"

"Yes, she's working on a project. I mentioned it was time, but she may need your assistance in arriving. How was your adventure?"

"It was awesome," Rob says, smiling. "It was as if you were with us. But I'll tell you about it later. Let me get everyone directed in here."

Jan and Peter are first to arrive. Debbie and Bob take the chairs closest to Sarabeth, with Laurel on the other side. Sophia runs over to kiss Sarabeth and then sits close to Rob.

With everyone seated, Sarabeth begins to organize the energy of the channeling.

"Let's focus our intention on what we want to experience and receive from the channeling. Bring your energy into this space by focusing your attention right here, right now. Take several deep, cleansing breaths and release all the day's activities as you exhale. Breathing in and breathing out. Imagine golden light entering the top of your head on your inhalation. Allow it to move down through your body, along your spine, and then out your feet and hands. As you exhale, release any nagging negative energy, feeling, or physical symptom. Continue breathing in and breathing out. From within your heart center set a loving intention for this channeling. Good! We are all vibrating at a high level."

Sarabeth takes a deep, cleansing breath as she begins her inner-directing mantra. "OK, let's begin:

"*Source energy, allow me to be a clear healing channel. I call in one hundred thousand angels to please come in and fill this room; I invite in only high-frequency light beings. Please come in to guide me and offer me interpretation for this fourth evening of this retreat on healing psycho-emotional trauma through the ancient traditions. Thank you for your protection and guidance dear Archangel Michael, Archangel Raphael, the Council of Twelve, Metatron, the Marys, Archangel Uriel, Archangel Gabriel, and Orion.*"

Sarabeth relaxes into her chair, feeling a deep love overwhelming her. She feels the voice and words from the channel. Her voice lightens and softens as she speaks the words, augmented by the complete knowing of what is being shared.

"Dearly beloved, we are here, and we want you to know how much we love each of you. It is a joy to assist you in bringing increased light into your vessels as you choose to have this experience. All is energy and light. As you focus your intention and attention on light, you open further to your healing capacity and to receive the historical traditions you desire. We are grateful for your ongoing focus and attention to the light and the integration of spirit, mind, and body. This is necessary for healing and health. To increase your integration process, focus your intention from an open heart center. In this way you are able to receive a higher frequency of light. Anchor this in your field through intention and connection to source. Ground yourselves into the earth as you rise up to source. You may imagine this as a light that moves through your chakra system and anchors into your field. As a reminder from previous channelings, you can think of this as if you are stepping into the light, and the light pours in, though, and around you.

"You have been learning that attention and intention focus energy and creation. And your dreams are giving you proof of this—that you create that which you put your attention to. Several of you have been having intense experiences in the dream state. Attending to joy begets joy. Focus on fear and you experience more fear and lacking. The space that many feel stuck in is that space between these two centers—between the two attentions. This creates stagnation, or a spiral of movement back and forth. It also blocks movement out of third dimension and the cycle of karma.

In order to enter or access the frequency of fifth, sixth, and seventh dimension you have to focus on joy, what you desire, and the light frequency of love. We have said that you choose your creation through your attention and intention, and love. And that love creates living; fear creates not-living. Fear cannot exist where there is love. Come from your heart space and you will be in the space of love, which allows for direct communication with spirit, compassion, and light. Breath moves stagnation and blocks. Focus your breathing. Allow in higher light frequencies and open yourself to light language. The use of color and toning assist with the lightening of the body, emotion, and spirit, the connection to high light frequency and source.

"We have discussed that breath-holding in reaction to fear can create a development of habitual dissonances, which, over time, can disrupt your connection to your integrated spirit, mind, and body, so that you lose your connection to yourself. Notice how the culture in which you live has driven spirit out of its place; driven nature out of her place with spirit. The common reference is to mind, not spirit...positioning spirit as an afterthought when indeed the guiding source point is from your heart space from spirit as leader, with mind creating what is presented from spirit.

This is the way, yet in your common vernacular, this has been rearranged. Doing so decreases and diminishes your light capacity. This is how negative need-based drives, the secondary drives, take over behavior in humans. This is a skewing of the not-living in the light; it is a skewing away from your essential being and life path. It is akin to holding your breath, blocking the flow in inspiration and expiration of energy, so that your self becomes bound and small. This energetic action is what creates all disease in your spirit, mind, and body. All disease begins from the perspective of 'shen' disconnection, from a spiritual disconnect within a being that then begins to contort and knot.

Trauma can be the first way that energy starts to disconnect. Because of the natural flow of energy being from spirit to mind to body, it can develop into distorted thinking, stagnation, and visceral and corporeal distortion. Over time, this distorts and knots the energetic flow around you. This blocks the light frequency available to you and creates a dulling of your senses, and a distortion of your perceptions. This can result in various forms of disconnections and can begin to be made tangible in the physical and cognitive fields.

"To enhance your ability to hold higher and greater levels of light we encourage you to create a practice of using healthy foods and removing toxins when strengthening your physical body to hold a higher frequency of light. Engage in the practice of yoga, qigong, spiritual mantras, daily meditation, and ceremonial and sacred use of plant medicines and herbs, aligning with the natural flow of the moon to strengthen your emotional and spiritual field and connection with the power of the elements of the wind, earth, water, and mountains.

"The energies of flow and allowing are key to increasing the frequency of light. Allowing each emotion its expression, with love and compassion, allows for it to be released, and you to be guided to your true essential being. If you have a history of trauma, these activities may not be enough. Focus your meditation on healing your connection to your fifth-dimensional blueprint and soul retrieval.

"One of the biggest blocks to this kind of flow and allowing comes from an experience of shock and trauma to the spiritual, emotional, physical system that goes unabated or which is not worked through. This requires clearance and integration to be assimilated. Lack of this clearance and integration leads to disease within the physical, emotional, and spiritual well-being of a being.

"Healing of such trauma comes from the release of the original trauma, a shift in focus of attention and intention, and a direct connection of light through the whole of the experience. This can be accomplished through guided meditation that incorporates a feel/see/know re-experiencing and reworking of the event, as well as specific acupuncture-assisted energetic release treatments. As offered in earlier channelings, this can be enhanced through the practice of meditation, yoga, mantras, guided visualization, toning with toning bowls at various hertz, flute music, rattles and singing, crystal energy, and the penetrating focus of love.

"Loving oneself fully and experiencing forgiveness heals. Elimination of the stagnating and harmful patterns, as well as elimination of the controlling patterns developed to assuage the pain, fear, and anxiety will assist in the release of the trauma, a return to balance, an opening to love, and forgiveness.

"Your thinking is connected to your emotional and spiritual and physical being, and when you are distorted within this integration, your thinking is distorted. This is an interactive system—each affects the other. You can heal your thinking through a reclamation of healthful living, cleansing your physical actions and behaviors with a focus on prayer and meditation, or you can heal your body through shifting your thinking, meditation, clarification, prayer, self-love, and loving-kindness.

"The earliest of treatises in the Taoist practices regarding healing and consciousness addressed these injuries. The cycle of give and take, increase and decrease, firmness and flexibility are all a part of how this natural process of flow and allowing works within the physical, emotional, and the spiritual. When something is stuck, sharply avoided, blocked, or cut off these processes are interrupted and unbalanced. These blocks, disconnects, knots, or lack of flow work like a dam and create an increasing imbalance. These imbalances result in disease and disordered interaction among and between your spiritual, emotional, and physical fields, resulting in aberrant behavior and an incapacity for holding high light frequencies.

"The practice of yoga can create a return to balance in the relationship of spirit, mind, and body. It is important to practice this as a whole-being experience, not just as exercise or focus on the asanas alone. Use of this practice is a way to focus on self-love and to release limiting beliefs and physical holding patterns.

"You can use toning, essential oils, healing herbs, and colors to activate a shift in one of the sensing fields—sound, smell, taste, sight, and touch—and offer a healing thread back to an integrated spirit, mind, and body. This process of using senses to shift toward a heart-centered connection is the most efficient way to release the blocks in the physical, mental, emotional, and spiritual bodies, as well as the etheric template from the individual's field. When you are focusing on release, always bring in light following, and then seal the new energy, otherwise you or your client are left open in a way that is not stable. You are a container of the light, and you need to allow an opening to the ground, earth energy, and the high light energy but not to rampant negative energy to static from others. To seal the container use flutes or singing, floral smells, or tinctures and light.

"The use of specific acupuncture points to focus release and redirect a stagnant flow is helpful. These strategies are subtle and go underneath the rigid holding pattern set up by the mind-body connection lacking spirit. This is especially effective through toning. With *the release of the block and a reconnection through the heart center, spirit is brought back into a balanced relationship within the person, and this shifts the situation at a quantum level. It looks like a miracle and yet is simply the clarification and amplification of what is not and what is, so that the integrated being may uplevel to a higher degree of harmony and balance."*

Sarabeth shifts in her chair. "Hang on, everyone, I have to go deeper for a new channel to come in. This is the Pleiadian energy." She reaches for another lozenge and closes her eyes.

"We want to talk a little about the importance of how to discern whether information you are receiving is from fear-based ego drives versus an intuition or energy from your soul, or source energy.

"Intuition or soul communication has a loving quality to it. It is light, subtle, and calming. It has force but the force is stable and not anxious in any way. Ego, fear-based thoughts, and communication are anxiety-driven and loud. You may feel yourself unable to think clearly, only driven by a single negative thought or fear. Pressure to act. You may feel electric, shaking, unable to calm yourself, or obsessive when you are driven to do something or take an action that is not an intuition. Intuition or soul communication lightly offers a way or path or information, without anxiety. You will feel expanded and calm. It is quiet and subtle. As you listen and accept the information, more will come, like you are opening a faucet so that water can flow. It will offer you peace even if the information is revelatory. When it is ego, fear-based, taking the action feels out of your control and does not bring peace—only more anger, fear, or a lack of control. Intuition and soul, source communication, feels you are on the right path and you feel peaceful and loving.

"We are aware that you have questions and would like to answer these to your completion. Several of us have spoken in this time, and many high light beings are ready to provide loving guidance and information for you. We want you to know how much we love you and how grateful we are to be your interpreters for this information.

"We are available for specific questions. Remember to drink plenty of water to assist your assimilation of this information at the

cellular level as you are integrating this information and increasing the degree and frequency of light you are each holding. Cleanse your energy field with rose geranium, eucalyptus, and sage, as well as baking soda; and allow yourselves plenty of rest to help with assimilation of this information. Always allow yourself some grounding foods, cleansing baths, or hot oil treatments. Even just running your finger along the meridian channels on the feet and around your neck can assist in this opening and grounding. You may be grounded through walking on the ground in your bare feet. Salt on the balls of your feet will assist to bring you into your bodies while simultaneously encouraging the anchoring of the light and new information.

"We are so pleased to have this opportunity to share this information and love you very much. We await any questions you may have."

Sarabeth lightly speaks.

"Thank you so much the Pleiadians, the Council of Twelve, Archangel Ariel, Archangel Gabriel, Archangel Raphael, Metatron, and Orion. I am so grateful for this information. At this time, I will open it up to questions... Please begin from my left."

Jan begins to speak.

"Can you discuss how to use the wu shen and the ghost points in healing psycho-emotional disorders? And can you discuss the use of food as medicine in this regard?"

"Hello Jan. We are very pleased that you have decided to ask this question. It is the completion of the discussion above. We want you to know that we love you very much and are deeply grateful to you for the persevering focus you have directed toward educating others in the responsibility of owning their path and living in a balanced manner.

The wu shen, or five spirits, are the immaterial aspect of the human being. They are the most ephemeral vibration of qi. They cannot be seen but are known through their support of all that is seen, heard, felt, understood, and known by the senses. The five spirits are sources within the human body for each aspect of spirit connected directly to the human body through the six senses, as intuition is the *integrated expression of the wu shen. These spirit whorls in the human body hold the space for the heart-centered spiritual guidance we have been interpreting to you, and it is through these centers that light can be strengthened and healing. They can be accessed through acupuncture via specific points, each moving from the most subtle shen to the most substantial.*

Whereas the five elements begin in the dark yin of water, the earth, the deep collective unconscious, the five spirits begin at the utmost light, yang, fire principle. They are the height of heaven, insight, inspiration, and dreams. The attraction and interaction of the yang to the yin creates the alchemical transformation. Shen, the spirit of fire, descends toward zhi, the spirit of water, descending into mind and body, manifestation, deep unconscious, and finally, the underworld of the collective unconsciousness. Zhi ascends toward shen; this is the way and the flow. This is how manifestation happens.

"As this is in balance, the human being is in balance, as there is imbalance, there is disease or distortion away from one's higher consciousness and soul path. To understand the disease and to know what and how to treat the imbalance, look at the story presented by the individual you are treating. This will guide you to the injury and to the spirit center that is disconnected, blocked, or not flowing.

"When there are issues of intuitive insight, inspiration, reason, thought, and conscious awareness, look to heal the shen spirit, look at the heart and pericardium, and the element of fire; ren 15 is the gathering point for this spirit. When there are issues with dreaming, imagination, and vision, look to the hun spirit, look at the liver and the element of wood; liver 14 is the gathering point for this spirit. When there are issues of direction, planning, ideation, intention, and action, look to heal the yi spirit, look at the stomach and spleen, and the element of the earth; gallbladder 24 is the gathering point for this spirit. When there are issues with incubation, instinctual responses, somatic awareness, emotion, or sensation, look to heal the po spirit, look at the lung, colon, or large intestine, and the element of metal; lung 1 is the gathering point for this spirit. When there are issues with manifestation, faith or trust, sexuality or reproduction, sleep, obsessions, desires, or apathy, look to heal the zhi spirit, look at the kidneys and the element of water; gallbladder 25 is the gathering point for this spirit.

"The wu shen give you a view into where the tear or skew in the spiritual system was set in motion, and a way in which to reset the connection.

"Your intuition and sense of the person will give you further clues. Pay attention to what you feel within your own body as you first come into contact with the person. You can gain a great deal of insight through your first sense awareness of the person. You will discover information that is hidden to the person in this fashion, but that can become an essential building block for their healing.

"Food is a medicine. To create healing through food, pay attention to how various spices can heal the specific centers involved. Taste is very useful. It can be effective in healing the spirit-disconnect. The energetics of the various foods can be incorporated to further assist the spirit center balancing. Use the colors associated with the five elements for each of the spirit centers to choose specific foods and styles of cooking, like long and slow to heal longstanding issues, and quick flash for vegetables when the spleen is injured, to heal and reclaim the health of the spirit. You can also use the seasoning of the five elements associated with the five spirits to assist in restoring balance.

"We are aware, Jan, that you have a great deal of knowledge in this arena of food. You can apply this to the sketch we have drawn for you to strengthen your healing strategies with food and toward the five spirits. If you were to meditate on each spirit center while you were quietly analyzing the individual's story, this would help you to get a clearer image of what foods will clarify the spirit or strengthen it.

"We want to shift interpreters to assist you with the use of the 13 ghost points. Please wait as we allow Sarabeth to transition into a deeper state for this next interpreter of information.

"Greetings to you, Jan. I have been observing your work with the ghost points for many years and see that you understand the theory behind these quite fully. I began my treatise on these essential points many centuries ago and you would refer to me as Sun Si Miao. My *observation is that phlegm, heat plus stagnation rather than angry spirits, interferes with the integration of spirit and cognition. So your theory that food can be helpful is a useful addition to the utilization of the ghost points because it can enhance the expulsion of the phlegm. Compassion in medicine is the utmost healer and without it no true healing is possible. When considering the use of the ghost points to release the phlegm and allow healing, understand there is indeed a deepening of disease over time and space. The four trinities of points offer a linear picture of when to use the specific points. Focus first on the symptoms presented; integrating this information with the five spirits allows for a depth and breadth in your treatment protocols. The thirteenth ghost point is essential in clarifying choice for the person being treated.*

"Burn-moxa on lung 11 and spleen 1 simultaneously assists in awakening the person to his path and opening his eyes to his soul's work. Needling pericardium 8 and large intestine 11 together allow for the individual to take steps to change his or her life in a transformational way. When you feel the person is holding onto the negative habitual style of being in the world, needle stomach 6 and ren 1. This will result in a deep clearing and opportunity to see how to act and a freedom to let go of the historical habit.

"Please consider this information and begin to develop your practice even further through meditation on these points. Use your inner intuition and see through your third eye. Use visualization when working with a person or guiding your students in their work. When you see the person from this inner plane, you can observe the disruptions in their field and see the interconnections of the five spirits within them. This will give you definitive information about what is the best treatment protocol. You have within you the capacity to see the human body complete and whole as spirit-human. You can use this skill to further define this healing field through your work and writing. We encourage you to document your work, Jan, so that it can be handed down to the generations that follow you. I am here for you whenever you need my assistance. You may call on me directly as you desire."

Sarabeth's voice changes slightly and she quietly completes the channeling.

"We are deeply grateful to you for this opportunity to share this information with you. We love you very much and want you to know that we are here for you any time that you want to call on us directly in these matters. You are a beautiful being on this planet. We wish you much love and light in your continued work on the planet. Does this answer your question sufficiently, Jan?"

Jan is quietly writing. She stops to wipe tears from her face.

"Yes, absolutely beautiful. Thank you very much for the information and your belief in me."

Sarabeth looks at the group.

"Do others have questions to ask today?"

The group is silent.

"OK, then, let's close off this session. Thank you all high light beings for your support and your information today. Each of you is of great benefit. Thank you all. Thank you Sun Si Miao. Archangel Michael, if you could clear the energy, thank you, thank you...With deep abiding love and gratefulness, thank you all...Kadosh, kadosh, kadosh. Om mani padme hum. Om, Gam, Ganapataye, namaha. Gate, gate, paragate, parasamgate, Bodhi, svaha!"

"What an amazing channeling. It is so interesting how we are getting these amazing historical figures. Their energy is quite different than that of Metatron, Orion, or even the Council of Twelve. The energy frequency is higher and yet they are more solid in some way. Perhaps this is because they connect to their selves in the physical to offer the interpretation about their work. The Marys have a similar feeling when they come through. The Pleiadian energy is so big and pure love, it's difficult to hold for very long."

Sarabeth drinks some water and eats some peanut butter.

"I feel very dizzy. Let's all drink a lot of water today to help with the assimilation of the information."

Sophia rubs the ball of her left foot.

"And we should eat peanut butter or chocolate, right, Mom?"

"Yes honey, that's right. You know the drill."

Sarabeth smiles at Sophia. Peter and Jan are still writing. Rob and Debbie appear to be quietly meditating. Bob looks at Jan.

"What do you think about the reference to you writing this all down for posterity? It's so weird to get such a strong recommendation from a spiritual guide, isn't it?"

"It's a powerful, challenging, and exciting experience to be sure, Bob," Jan says, smiling at the group. "I feel a little uncomfortable about the whole idea, actually."

Sarabeth smiles back at her dear friend. "OK, everyone, please remember to use some method of consolidation tonight; either through the apple cider vinegar baths with the sea salt and baking soda, or the hot oil treatments. Remember to have compassion toward yourselves and be gentle."

Rob gets up.

"Let's go eat. I made some wonderful stews and soups to help us ground and integrate. Come into the kitchen with me."

Rob takes Sophia's hand and walks out of the room. Slowly, everyone follows except Laurel. She stays back with Sarabeth, sitting quietly with her as she silently meditates about the information.

CHAPTER 9

The subtlest secret of the Tao is human nature and life (hsing-ming). The best way to cultivate hsing-ming is to bring both back to unity. The secret of how to cultivate both simultaneously was lost on earth. The seed matures out through the inner breath, the primordial pass moves into unity of consciousness and life.

Within the germinal vesicle is the fire of the ruler; at the entrance of the germinal vesicle is the fire of the minister; in the whole body, the fire of the people...When the fire of the ruler expresses itself it is redirected by the fire of the minister. When the fire of the minister moves, the fire of the people follows him...When the three fires return in reverse order, the Tao develops.

The thought which is powerful, the absence of thoughts, is Bodhi.

The thousand-petal lotus flower opens, transformed through breath-energy.

Because of the crystallization of the spirit, a hundred-fold splendor shines forth.

—The Hui Ming Ching/The Book of Consciousness and Life

Debbie is watching herself reach toward a doorknob. She is walking down a set of stairs and then a long hall. She sees herself go through door after door; she is getting nervous about the hallways and doors. Her attention is drawn to a woman crying out for help. She sees a light at the end of the hall, a door slightly ajar. Debbie enters the room. In the corner she sees a bed with a young woman lying there. She sees a light on and the woman is reading a book. As she steps closer, she sees it is her old friend who died many years before. She is smiling.

"Come in, Deb, it's OK. Come in. I've been reading about your work. It's amazing, everything that you have been doing since your studies in Santa Fe."

Debbie notices her name is on the cover of the book, and she sees other books, with other names on the covers.

"This is how I can see how my loved ones are doing, Deb. Each book is their book of life."

Her friend is holding one of the books very close to her. She is slightly hiding the name on the book. Debbie can make out the letter "S" and what looks like a "U," but nothing else.

"This one is very dear to me; she is struggling. I didn't expect it to be such a hardship for her. I thought her father would be able to help her more, but she has a stubborn streak—well, perseverance. And, she has such good intuition that she can tell when things aren't right. I didn't think of that. Debbie, I didn't think of that. Maybe because it hadn't shown up yet when I was with her. It developed after I had gone. I think it was one of the gifts of my leaving. Anyway, Debbie, I need you to help her. Help her to understand, to let go, and move on. She is stuck and I think it is making her sick. I can't go to her. I need her to understand from a grounded, human place. I need you to help me one more time. Will you help me, and help my dear one?"

Debbie watches herself go toward her friend and hug her. She watches herself say "yes." She watches herself take the book from her friend.

Just as she is turning over the book to see the name on it, she wakes up.

Two nights in a row, Debbie has the same dream. *I have to figure out why this is so important now*, Debbie thinks to herself.

Laurel is sweaty and slightly crying as she sleeps.

A very small child is walking down the hall of her home to her mother and dad's room. Sitting on the bed is her father; she looks at him. He is distraught, holding a pill bottle in his hand, shaking his head, saying over and over, "How did this happen? How did this happen?" The little girl looks over to her mother, who's limp on the bed, with a sweet, calm smile on her face.

The child goes to her mother and touches her arm. "Mommy, are you... ?" *She pauses; her mother's arm is ice cold.* "Mommy?"

"Daddy, what's wrong with Mommy?"

"She's gone, honey."

"No, Daddy, no! How could this happen? I need her to stay with me."

"I know, honey, I want her with us too; I know how hard this is for you. Don't worry, you aren't alone. I will be there for you twice as much now that you don't have Mom, and we'll keep her memory alive with love; come here, honey, let me hold you."

"Daddy, it's not fair, it's not fair. I want my mommy."

The little girl crumbles in her father's arms, crying in big heaves, then little sobs. She falls asleep with her father holding her.

Laurel awakens, her pillow soaked with tears again. Laurel talks out loud to herself. "I wonder if I just ask the channel about my dream, will I not have to share my primary reason for being here?"

Laurel shivers as she remembers the feeling inside her when she was in Debbie's field. She says to herself, "It's as if she had the energy of my mother. How can that be? How can we be connected at such a core level?"

Laurel pulls out the corkboard with all the bits of information and Debbie's name in the center.

"She has some weird connection to me, but what is it?"

Laurel lays her head back down on the pillow, and gently falls asleep.

Sarabeth and Rob are making coffee in the kitchen.

"Rob, I've been thinking about Laurel and her mystery. Do you think someone here is responsible? You never met her mom, right? I mean, before I knew you."

Rob looks at Sarabeth quizzically.

"No, honey. I don't think so. Unless it was when I was doing my painting internship in Taos. But surely I would remember someone dying. And her father would have remembered me at least. You know, when we met before he died. I don't think I'm the 'murderer' she is looking for. Honestly, I suspect it wasn't precisely murder but some kind of euthanasia—if it wasn't a mistake on her mother's part, because there is no motive for killing her. You know what I mean? There was no inheritance and no foul play, like an affair or something, that any of us know about. And she was so sick, she was going to die anyway."

Sarabeth touches Rob's hand.

"Yeah, I think that's true. But it's a mystery how it happened. And it seems to be driving Laurel a bit crazy. I hope she's able to find peace."

Sarabeth takes a drink of her coffee.

"Debbie is also struggling with the death of a friend. She said she was going to talk with Laurel about it."

Rob is cleaning the dishes as he listens to Sarabeth.

"Yes, I think you told me that when they did talk, Laurel was strangely affected."

"Yes! She said she felt like she knew the person when she got into Deb's field. It was like she could kinesthetically feel a familiarity but did not know who it was. And it totally freaked her out. She said she basically ran away from the meeting. It sounds odd, but I have had that feeling before—it is unnerving."

Sarabeth hands Rob her coffee cup to wash.

"I'm going to get ready for a run. What are you going to do?"

Rob finishes the last cup and puts it away. "Hmm, I'm not sure, actually. I think I may try to catch up with Bob and Debbie. I was interested in their take on how the collective unconscious and Jung's work dovetail with Taoist cosmology. Have a good run, honey. Love you."

Rob leans over to kiss Sarabeth. Sarabeth kisses Rob back.

"Thanks. Those two always have so much to say. You will learn a lot, I'm sure! Love you too."

Sarabeth leaves the kitchen and goes up the stairs to her room. While changing her clothes she stares out the window toward the mountain, thinking of Laurel and Debbie. *It's like they're in search of information about the same person. But how can that be?* In her mind, she sees a flash of an image. *Debbie holding a medicine bottle.* Debbie looks so different, so young. But she can tell from the energy that it is her friend. Her heart falls. She sees the flash again. She knows that they are intimately connected now. Shaking her head, she puts on her shoes, grabs Leo's leash, and attaches it to Leo.

"We gotta go, boy."

CHAPTER 10

Without beginning, without end,
    Without past, without future,
    A halo of light surrounds the world of the law.
We forgot one another, quiet and pure, altogether powerful and empty.'

The emptiness is irradiated by the light of the heart and of the heaven.

The water of the sea is smooth and mirrors the moon in its surface.

The clouds disappear in blue space; the mountains shine clear.

Consciousness reverts to contemplation; the moon-disk rests alone.

—The Hui Ming Ching/The Book of Consciousness and Life

Sarabeth is drinking a latte in the kitchen.

"Hi, Rob. I'm waiting for Lance to arrive. Have you seen him?"

Rob looks at his watch.

"Not yet, but I think it will be anytime now."

"I'm really excited to see him."

Sarabeth's eyes are sparkling as she brushes her hair back.

"I'm glad he is able to come to the last weekend of the conference. He's so busy now, with his trainings. I saw his TED Talk about his program to use the push-pull theory to integrate lessons from trauma through the energetic flow between people. It connects through mind the same energy we are learning about here: The connection between trauma and healing in a positive way."

Rob stiffens his back and rounds his shoulders, as he makes a new latte. The machine whirs behind him.

"It's difficult to think about that time when you two used to talk late into the night about that theory, and so many other things. I feel a knot in my stomach. You were so close to him then, I'm uncomfortable about what is to come with him being here."

Sarabeth is absentmindedly circling the top of her coffee with her finger. "It was a different time then, for all of us. Sophia was so little, so innocent. I'm glad we spared her from it all. She only remembers that he was her ice-skating coach. I know it brings up these painful emotions for you—for me, too. But so much has happened since then."

Sarabeth is thrown back into turmoil with the memory of her heart being torn in two directions. Memories of Lance's face, body, touch, voice flash across her inner vision. *I have missed him,* she thinks to herself. *I hope having him here doesn't blow up. Our energies are combustible when we are close.*

Rob looks on the monitor.

"Well, here we go. Please, Sarabeth, don't lose your way. I see him walking up from the gate."

Sarabeth looks into Rob's eyes. "It will be OK, Rob." She pauses momentarily to squeeze his hand, and then grabs her phone and walks to the door.

"Lance." Sarabeth reaches up to hug him.

Lance leans down and pulls Sarabeth off the ground.

"Hi, Beth! Let me look at you."

Leaning back, Lance looks at Sarabeth.

"You look so radiant. You have changed so much; your hair is so long."

Sarabeth hugs Lance again.

"You look so different too. I can feel your energy is much stronger and more aligned, and you actually look taller. Oh,

I have missed you, my dear friend. Thanks for coming! Wait until you see Sophia. She's quite a force now, really beautiful and strong, not the little girl you remember, I'm sure."

Taking Lance's hand, Sarabeth is overwhelmed by the images of being with him. Her body shakes uncontrollably. Lance stops and pulls her close. "Are you OK? I feel it too."

She turns back toward his face. "I forgot what it's like when we are near each other, how it feels we're in some place between worlds where no one else exists."

Lance reaches back and closes the door behind them. He places his shoulder bag on the floor near the door. "I've been waiting a long time to see you again."

"Lance!" Sophia is running down the stairs, two at a time. She jumps into his arms.

Lance warmly hugs Sophia. "Well, hi there. Look how big you are! Are you still ice skating?"

"Yes, I am. I just finished a show. Mom has a video." Sophia hugs Lance again. Lance looks up at Sarabeth smiling. "So, you have a video huh? Just one?"

Sarabeth guides Lance into the kitchen and invites him to sit at the counter with a wave of her hand.

"Yes. This time I only took one. Hard to believe, I know. So, you've become quite famous. How does that feel?"

Lance puts his hand on Sophia's shoulder.

"Your mom thinks I'm famous. What do you think?"

Sophia pulls up a chair next to Lance.

"I think you are too. Mom showed me one of your talks. You looked different, but it still sounded just like you. It was cool. How does it feel?"

Lance helps Sophia with the chair.

"Well, it's cool, I guess. It feels kind of the same as not being famous, so far. I'll let you know if that changes. But I'm kind of excited about your mom's work. How is it going, Beth?"

Lance gently touches Sarabeth's hand, catching her eye, and smiles. Sarabeth smiles sweetly back at Lance.

Squeezing his hand, Sarabeth says, "It's been a great week so far, lots of interesting channelings. Laurel is here. It will be fun for you two to reconnect."

Lance sips Sarabeth's coffee.

"I thought she might be here. You've been friends so long. What's new in her life?"

"She has some drama about her mom, but I will let her catch you up. She's working on a lot of good stuff right now."

Sarabeth leans in to look at Lance's face. "Your eyes look a little sad, Lance. Are you OK?"

Lance looks deeply into Sarabeth's eyes. "I'm good, Beth." And then whispers lightly, "You always see me." Lance gently brushes Sarabeth's hand as he passes her the coffee.

"How are you, young lady?" Lance shifts his attention to Sophia.

"I'm great! Do you want me to tell you about my dream? I think one of Mom's channels came to me to teach me something. Mom thinks I might be channeling too. Isn't that cool?" Sophia pulls on Lance's arm. "Come upstairs so I can show you."

"OK." Lance smiles over his shoulder at Sarabeth. "Is this your parents' house, Beth? It's so nice!"

Lance's voice trails off as Sophia pulls him up the stairs.

Sophia is showing Lance the information from her Chinese guide.

"Dad and I found this online and mom says it might be what I was dreaming about. Did I tell you about my dream?"

Lance is looking at the material.

"No, you didn't. What happened?"

"Well, I saw someone writing, and it was something special that he was writing, and then he hid it. And then, someone came in and killed him and stole the writing. It was really strange because they were speaking in another language, but in the dream, I knew what they were saying. Mom thinks it's because I was part of that time period long ago. Do you believe in past lives, Lance?"

Sophia stops what she was doing and looks at Lance.

"Actually, I didn't used to believe in them until I met your mom. She convinced me."

Lance looks pensively out the window.

"How did she convince you?"

Sophia pulls on Lance's arm to sit on the couch with her.

"Well, I think it was something that happened organically. It's like a feeling I had that just grew inside me until I realized I believed."

Lance looks at Sophia.

"Hmm, did something happen that made you feel that?"

Sophia sits back on the couch and leans into Lance's body.

"It was more subtle. I felt something inside me opening. It is kind of like I started to remember things that I didn't know I knew. It sounds weird to talk about. Your mom had memories too. We shared them and realized that we had a lifetime together long ago. Then more memories came as intense things happened between us."

Sophia sat up. "What kind of intense things?"

"Well, let me think about how to describe it."

Images of Sarabeth filled Lance's mind. Her naked body under his covers in his apartment; the smell of her hair against his face; rain pouring down on her as she stands outside his door; the weight of her body against him crying.

Lance focuses his attention onto Sophia as she is staring at him.

"You know intense emotions that surround events? I'm not sure if it was the events or the emotions, but flashes of memories would just happen in my mind. When we talked about it we realized we had lived many lives together. It made me feel closer to your mom in a way that was brand new to me. She said she had felt it from the beginning of knowing me but was afraid to share it. Over time it made our friendship deeper, more special. It was a difficult time in my life—I think your mom's love and help changed me so that I could grow and be who I am today. Do you remember when I used to call late at night and talk with your mom?"

Lance stops talking to wait for Sophia to answer.

"Oh yes, I do. I used to get mad because she was spending so much time with you. But she said it was important and that she had to help you—that you had an agreement from another time. Did she mean from another lifetime? Wow... that is really cool that you both could remember and act on those feelings."

Sophia smiles at Lance.

"I'm sorry I wasn't more supportive, Lance."

Lance squeezes her arm.

"Don't worry about it. It all turned out great. Look—we're here together, and everyone is happy."

"Are you happy, Lance? 'Cuz mom said back then you weren't happy, you were sad."

Sophia looks into Lance's face, searching to see if he's happy.

"Your mom helped me a lot then. I'm very lucky she loved me so much. She changed my life...I think I'm happy now. I'm finding my way for sure. I've missed your mom. But we had to end our contact for a little while so I could grow, and she could grow. It was taking up too much time for your mom to be there for me. I felt like she needed to go on with her life and do her work, to be with you. Over time I was able to make sense of things and find my way to my work, too. Sometimes you can be too close and it changes your vision. Do you know what I mean by that?"

Lance looks at Sophia, who looks confused.

Sophia shakes her head. "I don't think I understand that, but maybe I just haven't had those kinds of experiences yet."

"It makes it so you don't see the big picture and you miss out on what's really special. Once we had some time away from each other, I realized what a gift your mom had been to me. You're lucky you get her all the time, Soph."

Lance squeezes Sophia's arm. Sophia leans back into him again.

"I've missed you, Lance."

"I've missed you too, Sophia."

Lance sits up.

"Do you want to show me that video of you from your last event?"

"Yes, it's on Mom's phone though. Come on, let's go downstairs."

Sophia grabs Lance's arm and they both go down the stairs.

Laurel is sipping coffee in the kitchen as Lance and Sophia run by.

"Lance! What are you doing here? You look awesome!"

"Hey there! Sarabeth invited me for the last few days of the seminar."

Lance stops to give Laurel a hug, then lightly touches Sophia's shoulder.

"Hey, can we wait a minute to see the competition?"

Sophia gives Lance a sad face but gently nods, yes.

"Sure, I'm going to find Mom. Don't be long, OK?"

"OK. I love you, princess. I won't forget. We can do it before your mom does her channeling, OK?"

Lance gently squeezes Sophia's arm. Sophia hugs him. "OK... "

"Wow, I didn't know you were still in contact with Sarabeth," Laurel says. "It was so hard on her when you guys decided to take a break. She missed you so much."

Laurel waves Lance to sit at the counter.

"Have coffee with me. Catch me up on your life."

Lance sits down next to Laurel and pours a glass of water.

"I don't need any more coffee, but I'll have some water. It was awful for me when Beth went away. But I knew we had to separate. Life was too complicated. After a time, I met a lovely woman, and I felt like I could use everything I learned from Beth to have a better relationship. It was good."

"Are you with her now?"

"No, it had its time and then we decided to part, too. She was young, and I think I need someone who matches me more. That was the hardest thing: to learn to trust myself and feel confident that I could create a better, stronger relationship with someone more like me. Beth used to always say that. Oh, we would fight about it... " as he trails off, Lance's face brightens, and his eyes light up. "Beth could see so much in me. I was lucky."

"Yeah, Sarabeth is a gift, but also completely frustrating, right?" Laurel says, laughing and rolling her eyes. "Honestly, she loved you so much; it took her a long time to find that light in her heart without you."

Lance looks off, away from Laurel.

"Yeah, me too."

Then, looking back at Laurel, Lance says, "She saved my life. It was worth every frustration, every moment. I'm so happy to be here with her. And you too; so, what's the story about your mother?"

Laurel winces.

"Dang, you two—still no secrets between you I see."

Lance laughs.

"Well, you know how it is, we see through each other; I'm pretty sure that will never end."

"OK, well, I really believe there is someone here who is responsible for my mother's death. All the evidence points to Debbie; it's like I can't even breathe when I'm around her. And, well, you know how I am with ghosts; I feel my mom around her. What's confusing is that I also feel so much love around her. It isn't the dark, negative energy I feel when I can feel a ghost who has been murdered. It's completely confusing. How is she responsible for her death and yet my mother is so at peace with her? I'm hoping that something will reveal itself in the channeling. I've carried this so long, now I'm close to finding the truth and it still eludes me. It is almost like I'm avoiding it. Anyway, thanks for listening, Lance."

"Of course. Beth will uncover the truth; it's in her nature to heal and balance all things out of sync."

Lance reaches toward Laurel's hand.

"It will be OK. Try to trust."

Laurel brushes away tears and gives Lance a feeble smile.

"OK. I'm going to find Beth and Sophia and see what kind of progress Sophia has made on her triple loop jump. What time is the channeling? Do you know?"

"It's probably soon. She was going to do it early today. I think she wanted more time with you afterward."

Laurel grabs Lance's shoulder.

"Be gentle with her, Lance. She loses her way sometimes when it comes to you. Or maybe she finds it. Whatever! It's so powerful, her love for you. Be gentle with her."

Lance looks at Laurel.

"What a good friend you are. Don't worry. I would never hurt her. I would give my life for her. We both agreed to separate for the good of everyone involved. That was a difficult time, but it's a different time now. There has been a lot of healing on everyone's part, I think."

Lance walks out into the hallway and stops by the stairs. Laurel sees him shift his shoulders a bit and imperceptibly stop, as if to conform himself. Then she hears him call out for Sophia.

Lance walks into the den on the left.

"Ah, there you guys are."

Sophia jumps up and runs to Lance.

"Come here. I want to show you my latest routine."

Lance sits down close to Sarabeth. "Hey," he says.

Sarabeth smiles sweetly at Lance. "Hey. You ready to see our girl kill it?"

"Well, of course. How's the triple jump you have been working on, Sophia? Are you still more horizontal than vertical? I never know how you manage that."

"Hey! Don't be mean. You're not my coach anymore. You have to be nice." Sophia looks at Lance. "I know you're just teasing me. It's actually so much better. Look!" Sophia sits on the other side of Lance, and all three look at the phone together.

"OK, good job! That is the best you have ever been! How do you like your new coach? It looks like she is really helping you."

Lance hugs Sophia.

"I'm so proud of you. I miss being on the ice with you and hanging out with your mom, Sophia."

"I like my new coach. She is really sweet. She never teases me. But even with the teasing, you are definitely my favorite coach, Lance! We tried to keep some of the same components I had in the routine you taught me. I like the new music better, and she taught me different fancy footwork to really increase my scores. I really like the different spin at the end. I think I look graceful. What do you think?"

"You look great! Really good job, I'm impressed with your progress."

Lance puts his arms around Sophia and Sarabeth and hugs them as they sit on the couch.

"Gosh, I miss you two so much. It's good to be here with you."

Removing his arms, Lance adjusts his position to face Sarabeth. "You look so good, Beth. So, what's the plan for the channeling? Laurel said you're doing it soon. Is that true?"

Sarabeth catches Lance's gaze and smiles.

"It's really good to have you here. Your energy is so nice. I've missed it. The plan is to do the channeling soon. Actually, I should go meditate to get ready. I have you bunking in Rob's study so you and Sophia can be near each other. I thought we could go out on the balcony from there later to catch up more. Let me show you, OK? Where did you leave your bag? At the front door?"

Sarabeth stands up and starts walking toward the front door. "Come on, Sophia, let's show Lance where he is staying."

Lance looks at Sophia. "I think your mom is trying to get rid of me. Come on, you show me where I'm staying. Is it where we went to talk about the dream?"

"Yes, it's where we were earlier." Sophia starts dragging Lance toward the door.

As Lance passes Sarabeth, he stops. "Bye Beth." He lightly brushes her cheek, and whispers in her ear, "I love you, Beth. It's so good to see you."

Quickly he turns his attention to Sophia. "OK, let's let your mom do her thing." Just as he leaves, he looks back and catches Sarabeth's eyes.

"You bring out a lot of silliness in us Lance. OK, I'm right behind you."

Sarabeth climbs the stairs quickly and goes into her study at the top of the stairs.

Sarabeth sits on her couch facing the window. She calls Leo to sit at her feet.

"Leo! Hi there, big boy."

As she pets his head, she smiles. With Lance's face in her mind's eye, her heart feels so full of love. She immediately starts to see images passing through her mind. She sees herself, Rob, and Lance in different clothing that indicates Native American, early English, Atlantian, and Lemurian. The images are flashes; and she sees cordings of light between Lance and Rob and herself. The symbols and images indicate they are part of a soul group and have connected karmic timelines. Two stand out to her. She had seen them before, years earlier, when she was working through her relationships with Rob and Lance in this lifetime. One where they were actually a part of the mythical story of Camelot, Sir Lancelot, King Arthur, and Queen Guinevere; and one that included Laurel in Atlantis. Then, more visuals of Lemuria and Atlantis—these have only been revealed to her through the channel. These images came to her so quickly and with so much power. Then, the one from her first intimate encounter with Lance: she and Lance surrounded by stars and bright colors floating through space.

The channel Mercury talks of multidimensional timelines, how Lance and Sarabeth were destined to be together after Rob died, but when Sarabeth saved Rob's life she changed the timeline. Mercury talks about timelines and soul agreements and choice. Flashes of information pass through Sarabeth's inner vision. Her heart racing, she breathes deeply and opens her heart. She waits to see if there is more. The images fade. Tears, rolling down her cheeks, fall into her lap. Her heart is filled with enormous love. Thank you, Mercury, kadosh, kadosh, kadosh. Om, shanti, shanti, shanti.

Sarabeth opens her eyes. Forty-five minutes have passed. The rich golden light of sunset surrounds her like a blanket. She leans over toward the table, grabs some palo santos and a match and smudges herself, quietly praying while it burns. The smell fills her with peace. She stretches her arms out toward the floor, lengthening her spine. Her reverie is interrupted by a commotion next door. It's Lance and Sophia laughing and talking excitedly.

Rob knocks gently at her door.

"Hi. You OK in here?"

Sarabeth shakes her head. "Not really, no. I'm a bit overwhelmed. How are things downstairs? Are you ready for me?"

"Yeah, everyone is there except Lance and Sophia. It feels like there's a lot of electricity in the room. You really don't look OK." Rob gently touches her shoulder. "It's time."

Sarabeth reluctantly gets up from the couch.

"OK, I'm coming. I'll see you downstairs. I just need three more minutes."

Bob says to Debbie, "I wonder what's going on? This isn't like Sarabeth. She's always so excited for the channeling."

Debbie touches Bob's knee. "I can feel so much activity. Look at Laurel. She looks like she has a lot going on in her head, too. I wonder. Oh, here comes Rob—and who is that with Sophia?"

Rob, Sophia, and Lance take seats facing where Sarabeth will sit. Rob turns to the group.

"Hi, everyone. Sarabeth will be right down. Let's just breathe and meditate for a minute and clear all this electric energy."

Sarabeth enters the room from the kitchen and takes her seat.

"Hello, everyone. I was just getting some extra information about tonight's channeling. I know you can feel all the electricity in the air. I think there's so much activity because we are going to receive a large download of information not just for our minds and intellect, but also in frequency and light. So, brace yourselves."

Sarabeth's eyes lock with Lance; she feels so much love in her heart.

"Some of you may not know our friend Lance. He's joining us for the last few days of the retreat."

Lance gives everyone a slight wave. Sophia climbs onto the chair with Lance and leans into him, leaving the chair between Rob and Lance empty. Rob looks at Lance and Sophia sitting together. His heart falls.

Sarabeth puts a lozenge into her mouth and takes a deep, cleansing breath as she begins her inner-directing mantra. "OK, I can feel you are all centered; this may be slightly different than other channelings, so let's begin:

"*Source energy, allow me to be a clear healing channel. I call in one hundred thousand angels to please come in and fill this room; I invite in only high-frequency light beings. Please come in to guide me and offer me interpretation for this fifth evening of this retreat on healing psycho-emotional trauma through the ancient traditions... Thank you for your protection and guidance dear Archangel Michael, Archangel Gabriel, Archangel Raphael, Archangel Ariel, Metatron, the Council of Twelve, Orion, the Marys, and Mercury...*"

Sarabeth relaxes into her chair, feeling a deep abiding love overwhelming her. She feels the voice and words from the channel. Her voice lightens and softens as she speaks the words, augmented by the complete knowing of what is being shared.

"*Dearly beloved, we are here and we want you to know how much we love each of you. It is a joy to assist you in bringing increased light into your vessels as you choose to have this experience. Intention and attention in a light yet clarified way assists you to open further to your healing capacity and to receive the historical traditions you desire. Through this process you discover more fully how all is energy and light.*

"*We are grateful for your ongoing focus and attention to the light and the ancient knowledge found within. Integration of spirit, mind, and body are necessary for healing and health. To increase your integration process, experience a sense of allowing. To be at peace within, go into your heart center and open to love. From an open heart center you are able to receive a higher frequency of light. Anchor this in your field through intention and connection to source; you may imagine this as a light that moves through your chakra system and* anchors into your field. Think of this as if you are stepping into the light, and the light pours in through and around you.

"Remember that attention and intention focus energy and creation...you create that to which you put your attention. Pay attention to that which brings you joy, that which you desire, and this is what you will create. You choose your creation through your attention and intention and the energy of love. Love promotes the blossoming of life; fear condenses and constricts. Fear cannot exist where there is love. To open to love, take in a deep breath and fill your lungs. As you exhale, feel the air moving through your body. Focus your attention on your heart space as you feel the pulsing there and the exchange of air in your lungs. Open your mind. Drop your attention from your thinking to your heart space. It is your feeling, but it is feeling informed by compassion and a sense of security in love. Come from your heart space and you will be in the energy of love, in the space of love. This energy allows for direct communication with spirit, compassion, and light.

"You may use your internal sensory guidance system, your emotions, as a doorway for you to further understand and connect with the higher, lighter frequency. Integration of your spiritual, emotional, and physical bodies happens in the heart space when you allow your sensory guidance system to inform and direct your actions. This integration increases your capacity to hold the higher frequencies of light on the planet so that you may remain in connection with the way, with heart-centered guidance to create healing and miraculous change.

"To develop a relationship with your sensory guidance system, see yourself as spirit-human; through your sensing-emotional body, you connect to your spiritual. Then, as you let your spiritual aspect guide you, remain open to where the flow of your emotion brings you. Through this method of openness you will connect to higher and higher frequencies of light. Imagine this flow like a river, complete with different levels and currents. Note that the currents of anger and frustration are at the superficial level. When you allow yourself to float under the anger or frustration, you can get to the underlying emotional issue of lack, sadness, betrayal, abandonment, or loss. From this space, open your heart to allow in more light, a fuller experience of love, and you will see these deeper emotions transform. Follow this until you can get to a space of gratefulness and love. Now you are anchoring very high light frequencies; from here you can create a full and complete healing.

"The energies of flow and allowing are key to increasing the frequency of light. Allowing each emotion its expression, with love and compassion, allows for it to be released and you to be guided to your true essential being. From this space you can see what is in your best interest, and out of a natural inner guidance, be guided by what brings you joy. The continuum of control and allowing is connected to creation and ownership in your life path.

"We discussed in previous channelings the importance of whole foods, fresh water, movement, daily meditation, and clean air, breath. And that both excess and insufficiency create dissonance in the balance within, dull the capacity for light, and lead to disease within each person.

"Today's interpretation is on what drives the soul, spirit, and personality of a being. We see that a friend of Sarabeth's has joined your group and this has prompted us to begin today's interpretation. Each soul has a relationship to a group, and often comes into incarnation with a set of agreements to fulfill. This is a layered process and includes what is called 'karma,' or karmic agreements. Most, but not all, of what drives a spirit-human are these soul agreements made prior to incarnation.

There are different timeline dimensions and there are relationships from past and future lives, which affect what choices a being makes throughout her life. At its core, this is driven by the soul purpose of each spirit human. Each being may have some conscious knowledge of the agreements driving his or her decisions—or not. This is driven by the being's soul. The level at which she is connected to her soul agreements indicates the level of conscious awareness regarding these decisions.

In some circumstances, one being may have more knowing than another and this can create pain for the one with the knowing. With permission from you all, we can identify some of the choices you made in this lifetime based on your karmic and soul relationships with each other. We will pause to let each of you acknowledge that you are willing to share this information with the group.

Lance, Sarabeth, Sophia, and Rob, you four have several lifetimes together, which have affected the relationships you created in this timeline. Rob, Sarabeth, and Lance, you are very old souls; you have many lives together. Laurel and Sarabeth, you are together due to several powerful lifetimes and agreements in this one. Bob and Debbie, you are aware of agreements that brought you together, and Jan and Peter, we believe you, too, are aware of these, but we also see a relationship between Debbie and Laurel that is very powerful. Peter and Sophia also have a very old connection that is revealed to us. Are you all willing to share with each other these connections so that you can learn from each other? We will pause to let you discuss and confirm that this is what you desire for today's interpretation."

Sarabeth opens her eyes and looks around at everyone. "Well, what do you think?"

Rob speaks up first.

"Honestly, I'm anxious about sharing with everyone. Unlike all of you, I am just a painter. My connection to consciousness is only in the beauty of my drawings. "I know it is valuable, so I am open to bend to the will of the group."

Sophia looks at her dad quizzically, and then her mom.

"It seems kind of exciting to hear the backstory on how we all got together. What do you think, Mom?"

"When they offer a chance to stop an interpretation it usually means something powerful is going to be shared, but that it might be overwhelming for the person receiving the information," Sarabeth says. "I am somewhat aware of what will be spoken about my karmic and soul connections, so it isn't too scary for me. How do the rest of you feel? Should we proceed?"

Sarabeth then gazes protectively at Lance.

"You OK with this?

Lance smiles.

"I'm OK, Beth."

Laurel looks at Debbie.

"I'm just fascinated to hear I have a connection to you. Do you know what it is?"

Debbie shakes her head.

"I have no idea. I am excited to learn about this, though. I've been studying this idea of karma and past lives for a while, and wonder how it's going to be presented in relation to emotional health."

Sarabeth looks at the group. "So, is everyone OK?" She looks at each person as they nod yes. "OK, I'll go back in."

"Thank you. We will continue. Time is not what you think it is. It is not linear. We speak of it that way to conform to your perspective of it in the third dimension. The fourth dimension is the space from which karma arises. Once you get into the fifth dimension you see that spirit is the powerful creator. You are made up of the tapestry of your and your ancestors' lives: It is woven in what you think of as your DNA.

For many of you, access to this is blocked in a cognitive way. It directs you through emotion, your senses, what you feel as something subtle driving you toward a relationship or connection. We spoke in a previous channeling about the fifth dimension of consciousness. You each have fifth-dimensional selves assisting you. Begin in this dimension to see time as all happening simultaneously. The future and past have a spiraling quality to them. You can see these aspects of yourselves as your high self: the soul overlay who is still connected to your soul group and who comes from a space of pure love and exists directly connected to source.

You can access your fifth-dimensional self via meditation. Sarabeth has been doing this for many years and often works at the fifth-dimensional level to bring in light for herself, those she loves, her clients, and the universe. She has worked with the Council at higher levels of seventh, tenth, and eleventh dimension. It is from this perspective that she assisted Lance to change his life. And it was from this perspective that she understood that she and Lance had come to this plane via a spacecraft made of light; they were twin connections of the same flame from a star system outside this galaxy. She saw that they came to this planet to heal the planet through their relationship. Lance had less understanding of this in his consciousness, but at a deep level he was able to access these images through meditation. Although not a painter, he was drawn to paint these images.

"Working in fifth is one of the most powerful ways to access source and create health, turning back disease to the proper flow of energy. Sarabeth and her friend Abby Wheat have been doing this work for several years now. To understand the power of the fifth dimension of healing you have to be willing to accept that alignment with spirit and your spiritual path is a direct connection to source. You must let go of your mind being in control and be at peace with the concept of one source of light. The part that usually blocks this is attachment to mind, and the illusion of control, and the personality you call the ego.

"Let's discuss timelines first. Time is all happening at once. It is like string theory from physics: many happenings at the same time. The being has the ability to comprehend between one and five happenings at a time. So, for those stuck in third dimension, the idea of birth and death and linear time is the only possible perception. As one opens to this idea, there are possibilities of past lives and future lives along the linear continuum.

Today we can discuss how previous connections created a drive to repeat that story among Rob, Sarabeth, and Lance. Sarabeth has had many lifetimes with Rob and Lance. We will speak of two lifetimes where there has been a triad between Rob, Lance, and Sarabeth. The energy of the mythical Knights of the Round Table, and the story of the love between the two knights, King Arthur and Sir Lancelot, and Queen Guinevere is the most accessible way to show how these get repeated. Rob, Lance, and Sarabeth have had many lifetimes working through this triad of love. And what we are trying to show you is that *the resolution in this lifetime can affect the past and the future as you see it in third and fourth dimension.*

For example, in this lifetime, Lance and Sarabeth had agreed to be together. Rob and Sarabeth also agreed to come together to bring in Sophia, and she was to be tied to Lance as well. Rob was going to leave early, and so Lance would come in to be with Sarabeth. Lance was to connect to both Sophia and Sarabeth, and their love was to help him align with his true potential. However, Sarabeth shifted this timeline through her lifesaving action toward Rob. This was a shift in her consciousness and her conscious source actions. It came from an opening in fifth so that the karma was shifted: The shift caused a deep reverberation. Lance grew through the love of Sarabeth and the connection with Sophia. However, Sarabeth and Rob remained connected.

"Laurel and Sarabeth, Rob, and Lance, you were all in Atlantis and involved in the big bang of transition of that culture. Sarabeth and Lance had connections with Lemuria and worked together on the integration of the two civilizations, a type of peace talks between these two cultures; whereas Laurel and Rob were only involved in the civilization of Atlantis.

"Laurel, you and Debbie are connected through your mother. We are aware that you have felt this energy when in her presence. This is a very strong timeline for you. It seems that Debbie interfered with the timing of your mother's passing. This has catapulted you on a journey of self-awareness and self-discovery. The relationship between you, Debbie, and Laurel's mother, Ruth, was quite strong and loving. You had been sisters and lovers in previous timelines. This is why, in this timeline, you and she had a short, very mean-ingful relationship when you were young. It is unlikely that Laurel or Bob have any knowledge of this. So this is why she called on you to act outside your nature when she was very ill. We will pause for a moment for questions."

Sarabeth opens her eyes and looks at Laurel. Laurel is stunned. She is looking at Debbie across the room.

Debbie begins to speak.

"Your mother is Ruth Hart? I don't understand. I thought her daughter's name was different. I am so sorry, Laurel; your mother was such a light on the planet and in my life."

Laurel is having difficulty finding the words to speak. She is filled with several emotions at once, unsure which to communicate out loud.

"This is why I felt my mother's energy around you. I knew you were somehow connected to her death. I thought you murdered her, but when I listen to the channel and feel your energy it doesn't fit. Why did you want to ask about my mom when we were at the dig?"

Debbie speaks quietly.

"I started having dreams about your mom the first night we arrived. In them, I saw your mom. It must have been some aspect of her soul; she was deep in my subconscious. She had these books, like books of the lives of the people she loved, those who were here on this plane. She was so worried about her daughter. I guess that is you, but the name on the book started with 'Su.' She thought that by creating a mystery to her death, a presumed accident, that you would be able to move on. Instead she said you became obsessed with finding out how it happened and who was the culprit. She asked me to help you. Again, I didn't realize it was you. I am so sorry, Laurel."

"My mom called me Sue, but I have always gone by Laurel, even when she was around. Very few people know me as Sue, not even Sarabeth."

Laurel's voice trails off.

"I feel like we should talk more, but maybe privately, if that is OK?"

Debbie nods. "Of course. I want to be helpful in any way I can."

Sophia leaves Lance and goes over to Laurel. She crawls in next to her and gives her a hug.

Sarabeth looks lovingly toward her two friends, and then at the entire group.

"So, do you want me to continue channeling? Do you have questions for the channel? Or would you like me to close off this offering for tonight? What do you think?"

"Perhaps we should see if there is anything else the channel wants to share today?" Peter says.

"I do have a question, if Laurel and Debbie feel they'll be OK to continue," Lance says.

Rob nods. "Me too."

"OK, I'll go back in."

Sarabeth closes her eyes, shifts in her chair and takes a few deep breaths. She begins to speak the words from the channel in a quiet, gentle voice.

"We are grateful to continue. There is so much to share on this subject of soul connections, karma, and timelines. This will be the continued focus of the next few offerings. We are aware that you have questions and would like to answer these to your completion. Several of us have spoken in this time, and many high light beings are ready to provide loving guidance and information for you. We want you to know how much we love you and how grateful we are to be your interpreters for this information.

"We are available for specific questions...remember to drink plenty of water to assist your assimilation of this information at the cellular level as you are integrating this information and increasing the degree and frequency of light you are each holding; today it may be best to cleanse your energy field with asafetida and frankincense as well as salt; and allow yourselves plenty of rest to help with assimilation of this information. Grounding foods will be essential. You may ground by walking on the earth or grass in your bare feet. Salt on the balls of your feet will assist to bring you into your bodies while simultaneously encouraging the anchoring of the light and new information.

"We are so pleased to have this opportunity to share this information and love you very much...We await your questions."

Sarabeth lightly speaks.

"Thank you so much Mercury, the Council of Twelve, Orion, the Marys, Archangel Ariel, Archangel Raphael, Archangel Gabriel, and Metatron. I am so grateful for this information. Please, whoever is ready, you may ask your questions."

Rob speaks first.

"I want to ask about a connection between Sarabeth and my son, Michael."

"Rob, thank you for this question, as it allows us to offer another way in which soul groups are connected. You and Sarabeth have had many timelines together, not just the ones discussed above. Some of these have included your son, Michael. Sarabeth has had several timelines as Michael's mother as well as his partner. In this lifetime, Michael and Sarabeth were drawn to each other as mother and son. The most recent life shared between them was in America in the middle 1800s, where soldiers in the battle at Little Bighorn killed Sarabeth and Michael. Sarabeth has a strong memory of holding Michael as a baby in her arms as they both fell to the ground, shot. When the ending of the timeline is intense in this way, the souls have a quality of recognition in their senses when they return; a feeling of déjà vu. Sarabeth and Michael were drawn to each other as mother and son. This was a powerful pull for them and led to a strong tie for Sarabeth and you. Does this answer your question, Rob?"

Rob nods. "Yes. Yes, thank you."

"There is another thing we want to share with you, Rob. You and Lance have had two lifetimes together that directly affect this lifetime. We see that your last lifetime was during World War II. You were a prisoner in the concentration camps and died a very painful death of starvation. We are aware that you have frequent nightmares, as if you are living through this drama over and over.

Lance also has these nightmares because you and he were there together. He used to bring you food. When this was discovered, he was killed. He has deep memories of being pursued, tortured, hiding and being found, and the painful death that followed. Over and over, these dreams come to him. It has had a profound effect on his sense of courage in this life timeline. This was a karmic agreement for him to give his life for you. You have three previous timelines in which Lance has sacrificed his life for you. Because of these timelines and those you share with Sarabeth, you have several agreements that are at cross purposes in this lifetime, and it makes you unsure as to what is the best thing to do in your relationship with Sarabeth. We encourage you to act from your soul center toward its highest goal. This is an example of where the secondary drives of the personality can interfere with the soul guidance. Finding peace will require you facing your fears and moving to divine love and forgiveness. Is this helpful information, Rob?"

Rob, stunned, shakes his head, removes his glasses and looks over at Lance for a long time, then focuses on Sarabeth. "Yes, thank you."

Lance leans back in his chair and runs his hands through his thick brown hair, looking at Rob. They exchange a nod. Then he turns his gaze toward Sarabeth.

"Beth, may I ask a question?"

Sarabeth opens her eyes and smiles at Lance. "Of course."

Lance continues to look forward, thinking how he wants to phrase his question. "I'm trying to understand the soul and timelines and how we are different but also the same...So, I guess my question is, can you have conflicting agreements, and are you made up of the same exact soul or is there some recombination of energies or entities? And how does the whole star aspect of the being play into it? You know how Sophia is from the Rainbow constellation but also has a connection to Liu Ruyi." Lance looks at Sarabeth. "Do you understand what I'm trying to ask?"

Sarabeth smiles broadly and nods yes toward Lance, then begins to speak.

"Lance, welcome to this group. It is most appropriate that you are here for this interpretation. We are aware of your work on the planet. Your work carries strong light, language, and interest to a new generation about consciousness, self-realization, and authenticity.

This is increasing the frequency of light on the planet. Your question brings a light mirth into the heaviness that has surrounded this channeling. This lightness allows for the information to come in deeper. We are grateful to you. You, Lance, are part ancient from another star system who's here to heal the planet, and part human soul with these previous lives discussed earlier connected to Rob and Sarabeth. And then you have a connection to Sophia and Sarabeth, and you carry something that we call 'angel energy.' You can create out of attention and intention, transformation, and transmutation just like Sophia. Are you aware of this latent talent in your energy?"

Sarabeth opens her eyes and looks at Lance for an answer.

Lance looks back. "Oh...that wasn't rhetorical. No, I had no idea I had such a talent."

"It is one of the reasons that you and Sarabeth are so connected because part of your soul plan is to help Sophia develop these talents. Certainly, you recognize that you have a strong connection to Sophia separate from Sarabeth; it is why your first contact with her was as a sports coach. It was the true vibration of your role in her life to coach her through developing this talent you both share. It is within you, and it is a result of the combination of energies that you came into this lifetime with. As you do this work of intention and attention, increased enlightenment following your soul path, and focus, you will see how to manage this talent so that you can use it to elevate consciousness on the planet. This is especially evident when you are using toning bowls and drumming to align and heal individuals' hearts in these groups. We see as you develop this and guide Sophia, you and Sarabeth will also become aware of work you are destined to do together. Does this answer your question, Lance?"

Lance speaks quietly. "I think I understand. I'm still stuck on the fact that Sarabeth told me this so long ago and I didn't understand how powerful this all is. Thank you."

"We see it growing in you, the strength to move this forward. Your work uses sound in a way that helps to open the meridians so that the individual has access to their fifth dimensional blueprint.

This allows them access to their soul path. We know you have been feeling the power that runs through you when you do this work, and it has been confusing you. It is our hope this information can bring you peace and renewed strength of purpose."

Lance sits back in his chair.

"That's true...how I have been confused. Thank you."

"Sarabeth, can I just ask a follow-up question to Lance's question?" Peter says quickly.

Sarabeth smiles at her friend. "Of course."

"Thanks. So the other day, after Liu Ruyi spoke to Sophia in the channeling, Jan and I were meditating, and I just wondered if there is a kind of spiritual DNA. The way we think of heritage, physically—is there a spiritual or star-aspect DNA or heritage? I kind of felt that was part of what Lance was getting at in his question." Peter sits forward in his chair anticipating the answer.

"Yes, Peter, there is a type of spiritual and celestial heritage. And each soul being can carry many aspects when in a timeline. So a soul can carry heritage, that is, from a civilization or aspect of a being. This is how Liu Ruyi can be connected to Sophia; and Lance can be part angel and star being and human soul. Sarabeth carries an ident of Mary Magdalene, and there are thirteen individuals on the planet at this time who carry such an ident.

"Peter, you and Sophia carry the same connection to Liu Ruyi. You were drawn to study him and his family through the inner guidance of your soul. We will stop now, as we see that Sarabeth is greatly fatigued. Thank you for your kind attention and interest."

Sarabeth gently wipes tears from her eyes. "Thank you, all high light beings, for your support and your information today. You have offered so much today, thank you all. Archangel Michael, if you could clear the energy, thank you, thank you. Kadosh, kadosh, kadosh. Om shanti shanti shanti."

Sarabeth looks at her friends.

"How are you all doing? That was a very long reading, and the information was so personal. This can be overwhelming. Take a breath."

Sarabeth breathes out and in several times.

"It's been good," Bob says.

Rob is looking down, his hands in his lap, tears in his eyes. Sophia crawls into the chair with him. "Daddy, what's wrong?"

"I think I just feel sad about some of the things the channel shared with us."

Jan looks at Sarabeth.

"It is so much bigger than I could ever imagine. Thank you for bringing this to us. How do you use this information in the treatment of psycho-emotional services?"

"Well, do you remember the information about how trauma causes the spirit to skew out? When I am working with the wu shen, the five sprits, I simultaneously move into fifth dimension and look to see the connections in their soul path to unwind the bundled cords that are blocking their soul's expression."

Peter reaches over to hold Jan's hand.

"This is extraordinary. I'm shocked to discover my connection to Liu Ruyi."

"I want to walk for a bit to see if I can integrate the information," Debbie says. She then brushes back her blond hair and reaches over to Laurel. "Do you want to join me?"

Laurel smiles at Debbie. "Yeah, sure."

Lance walks over to Sarabeth.

"Hey, do you want to show me the dig everyone is talking about?"

Sarabeth looks over at Sophia and Rob, then back to Lance. She feels torn.

"I'm going to see how Rob is doing. I know it was a lot, what they said. Are you OK?"

Lance sits down next to Sarabeth.

"Yeah, I'm OK. But you look upset. I know it was a lot for you, sharing all that, bringing it up again with Rob and me here together. It has to be difficult."

Lance touches her knee. Sarabeth leans her head on Lance's shoulder.

"Having you so close makes me feel unsure of our decision—what the channel said about our work." Sarabeth's voice trails off. She turns her face to Lance and whispers, "I'm not sure we made the right choice."

Lance puts his arm around Sarabeth and hugs her.

"I love you. We will find our way through this."

"I've missed you so much," Sarabeth whispers. She pulls away as she hears Rob and Sophia in the kitchen. "I think I need to check on the others. Will you be OK?"

"Of course. We can talk later. I'll be in the study."

Lance gets up from his chair, walks toward the front entrance of the living room, and stops at the door. As Sarabeth goes toward the kitchen, he looks back at her. As she enters the kitchen, she looks back toward him.

CHAPTER 11

I n a priori each thing has its own name that it can share
with you if you listen.
  —*Kototama Futomani*, Inochi: The Book of Life

The union of the yin and yang is the whole. This is the way, the Tao.
If the human mind lacks the mind of the Tao, it can defeat the Tao by
using consciousness to produce illusion. If you govern it by the mind
of Tao, the conscious light is clear and can thereby help the Tao. So the
mind of Tao is not to be diminished, and yet the human mind is not to
be annihilated; just do not let the human mind misuse consciousness.
When the ancients told people to kill the human mind, what they
meant was to kill the false consciousness of the human mind, not kill
the true consciousness of the human mind.
  —*Liu I-Ming*, Understanding Reality

Here the desirable relation of human mind and the mind of the Tao,
the earthly and the celestial, yin and yang, is one of subordination of
the former to the latter.
  —*Thomas Cleary*, The Taoist Classics

Debbie reaches for Laurel's hand as they walk toward the
dirt mound.

"I want to tell you a little more about my dream.
Remember when I said your mom was in this room
surrounded by these books? And how I think they were
books of the lives of different people she loved? I didn't
see mine, but she referenced it. I wanted to tell you about
the energy I felt in the dream. She was holding your book,
and it was so tender how she was talking about how she

made a mistake to go in the way she did. I just thought you might want more information about what happened that day.

"She had been in so much pain. She felt she couldn't endure it anymore, and she didn't want you and your father to watch her suffer. She really thought that you would be at peace and move on. But then she said in the dream she was somehow able to not just see your actions but feel your emotion, so she became aware of the pain you felt about the dissonance of what they said about her death and what you felt was true. She wanted me to help you. She gave me the book with your name on it in the dream, but, of course, it's not tangible, so I don't have it. When I awoke, I had no idea how I would find you."

Laurel stops walking and turns to face Debbie.

"But how is it that you know all this if it's just a dream? I don't understand."

Debbie takes Laurel's other hand and looks into her eyes.

"It's more of an access to a different realm, because I was able to actually talk with your mom as spirit. It's not just my unconscious sorting through what I know about what happened. It is kind of like how you see, feel, and hear ghosts. She is following your life. She has been the whole time. She is with you."

Laurel looks into Debbie's eyes.

"It has felt like she was murdered; but then when I felt your energy at the mound I could feel her on you, and I could feel so much love. It's difficult to acclimate to the change inside me about what happened. Can you tell me what happened? Like, how did my mom really die?"

Debbie lets go of Laurel's hands and looks away. She looks back at Laurel with tears in her eyes.

"Your mom contacted me and asked me to come down to see her. I hadn't seen her in many years: I didn't even really know about you and your dad until I got there.

"She was so weak when I got to her. She told me about you and your dad, and she asked me to grind up the medicine to give it to her as a double dose. She was sure it would release her from the pain, but that it would be gentle so that your father would just find her gone, as if in her sleep. I ground up the pills and gave it to her in a teacup with a little milk and honey. Your mom was so strong. She was determined. We shared a moment saying goodbye, and then I left. I read of her death being accidental in the newspaper later that week. And that is it. It was a simple action that irrevocably changed us both."

Debbie takes Laurel's hand again.

"I'm so sorry for how it has created such a rift inside you. Your mother was certain that you would heal faster if it was done this way."

Laurel squeezes Debbie's hand.

"I understand now. I think I can find peace with it and move on. I'd like to stay connected with you, Debbie; I mean, after the retreat is over. I would like to know my mom through your eyes, when she was young. Is that OK?"

Debbie hugs Laurel.

"Oh yes! That's more than OK. Let's go over to the mound and see what we find. Maybe a treasure to cement this moment."

Sarabeth smiles at Lance while she foams her milk. He begins to speak and then stops.

"You can't hear me over that machine; I'll wait."

Sarabeth turns off the machine. "OK, I'm done. What did you want to say?"

Lance walks over to her, takes her hand and says, "I just want to say I miss you. I miss our talks. Listening to the channel about how we're connected, it is so difficult to not be with you."

Sarabeth leans into Lance; she breathes deeply.

"I love the way you smell. I feel like a teenager ready to swoon when you're this close to me. It takes all my strength to not be with you. I'm so grateful for how I got to be with you for that short time. You changed me. Made me so much better. I love you so much. But it's not just us, it's them. I can't have Sophia hate you. She loves you so much now. You are hers and she would feel so much that she can't understand if I left her dad to be with you. These soul contracts are difficult when we are here in third dimension, don't you think? I mean, it makes sense you and me when we are multidimensional, but in third there is so much against us."

Her voice trails off. She holds Lance for a long time.

"I love you, Beth. I will always love you."

Lance gently kisses her head as he holds her in his arms.

"Do you love him the way you love me?" Lance whispers as he holds her.

Sarabeth pulls away. She looks into Lance's eyes. "No, it is different. I do love him. It's easier in many ways. With you it is like every cell of my being is lit up. Each time we're together I feel myself here and also in the stars flying. It is as if I'm channeling but it's more. It's like I am in the higher dimensions while simultaneously feeling all the passion in my body. It's indescribable. There was another for you. I saw her. She is so lovely. I didn't want to make this choice to not be with you. But we decided together, remember? We both decided together."

Lance takes Sarabeth's hand and looks at her fingers in his.

"She is lovely. And I enjoyed being with her, but something was missing." Lance turns over Sarabeth's hand in his. "She didn't fit the way you do. When I was with her, I kept feeling you. Your touch, your care, your crazy big mind and heart. No one can replace you in my heart."

Sarabeth looks up into Lance's eyes.

"Oh, how I love your eyes."

She reaches up moves his hair away from his face and kisses Lance. They embrace. Tears are running down Sarabeth's face.

"We have to let go. It's been too long. Someone is going to come into the kitchen. Too many people are here."

Lance gently moves away, still holding Sarabeth's hand. "OK. I know. I won't be alone. I just want to be with you. With everything we heard from the channel I know we agreed, but I wonder if it really is better for this timeline?"

Bob enters the kitchen.

"Hi, you guys, have you seen Debbie?"

Sarabeth lets go of Lance's hand and picks up her latte. "Hey, Bob. I don't think she and Laurel have made it back to the house yet. What's up?"

"I've really been trying to understand the timelines and the soul agreements and see how it fits with the collective unconscious of Jung. I thought maybe she could tell me what she thinks about it. But I guess she's still overwhelmed by the whole thing with Laurel and her mother, Ruth. I remember Debbie mentioning Ruth. But, of course, I never knew about this."

Bob starts to walk over to the latte machine.
Sarabeth and Lance walk over to the counter and sit down facing Bob from the other side.

"We can talk with you about it, Bob, if that helps."

"OK, sure, so here's what I was trying to put together. There's the stuff about the five spirits and heaven and earth that the channel talked about, right? And then there are the frequencies of the light body and the different dimensions like third and fourth and fifth and so on. And then there's the evolution of the soul and soul groups, and they're partly connected through DNA as we know it, and then also some sort of 'celestial DNA.' So...how do all of these actually fit together so that we can use it for healing?"

Sarabeth smiles at Bob.

"Yeah, it is a lot. I know."

Lance starts to speak.

"Bob, I'm not a psych person like you. I can be irritatingly logical if you ask Beth. I'm kind of a math person, and I think a lot of what Beth is talking about has been proven in math—well, in physics; you know, like quantum theory and string theory, how it is shifting time and space. There is a lot of work showing that time and space are not the way we experience them—or rather because we think of them in a certain way, which is how we experience them. But actually, time is not linear, and matter is far more than we have been taught—filled with holes, so to speak. Do you know what I'm referencing?"

Bob starts the latte machine and turns around. He comes over to the counter.

"Yes, I've read some of this."

Lance leans toward Bob.

"So, when it comes to dimensions and time and space, one plus one doesn't always equal two if you start to use quantum theory to show shifting in time and space. For example, the relative position of speed and mass and energy changes in certain circumstances. The ball thrown 25 miles an hour on a train going 100 miles an hour—relative to the train, the ball is going 100 miles an hour plus 25 miles an hour. One plus one. However, if the train is going at the speed of light and the ball is being thrown at the speed of light, then the ball is not going at the speed of light plus the speed of light. The math shows that mass moving at the speed of light squared creates energy, $E=mc^2$. Einstein's theory of relativity, right? But then the whole issue of vantage point came in and Einstein concluded that simultaneity is relative; events simultaneous for one observer may not be for another. And so, time flows differently for different observers; meaning an object in motion experiences time dilation. Einstein's work seemed to predict relativity well for large objects but less well for subatomic activity. That was better explained through quantum mechanics. Quantum theory shows shifting in time and space. The unified field theory, which tries to bring these together, is string theory. String theory postulates that extra dimensions of spacetime are required to make it work mathematically: Some say ten, others say 26. At any rate, this starts to identify that space and time are different than what we can perceive in third dimension with our senses, which is up-down, left-right, forward-backward, and time."

Bob grabs his coffee.

"I get that—well, mostly. But how are you applying that to my question?"

"OK, maybe that's too much. For our purposes, classical physics cannot explain consciousness, but quantum consciousness offers a way in."

Lance looks at Sarabeth and then back at Bob.

"Well, we're trying to understand these various concepts through third- or fourth-dimension paradigm and I think that doesn't work. Our consciousness needs to be in a fifth-dimensional space to understand what the channel is offering."

"Agreed." Bob says, sipping his coffee. "I think this is absolutely connected to the collective unconscious and I can tolerate the idea that we are living different timelines at the same time, and that time can bend in on itself—and, well, space too; I mean, I get that abstractly. I guess I need more of a structure to put everything in so that I can use this information to actually help people elevate their consciousness and heal. Do you think we need to actually elevate the consciousness of the planet for these shifts to be more self-evident?"

Sarabeth looks at Bob with a big smile.

"In my applied eco-psychology studies, my mentor, Mike Cohen, talked a lot about the unified field theory—not in the terms you're using, Lance, but he called them webstrings. He identified energy and consciousness in all things, plants, animals, humans, the elements of air, wind, land, rocks, everything; more like what we heard about from the Taoist teachers and what the channel talked about in the first few days, and all the information regarding the five spirits and the collective unconscious. I know when I'm working on someone in fifth dimension it doesn't feel like it does right now with us here. It's different."

Bob slowly nods his head in understanding.

"So, when the channel is suggesting bringing more light into our vessel, our beings, and using the acupuncture points to open the etheric template, it is telling us to move into these higher dimensions to bring about healing. And that the emotional and spiritual and physical traumas are what block people from healing—they create limiting beliefs and adaptive behavior that actually cause the being to not heal or stay stuck. Fascinating. I think I understand now. Thank you both so much."

Bob takes his coffee and walks out of the kitchen.

Lance looks at Sarabeth. "So is that what you do in fifth when you work on someone?"

"Kind of. It's multilevel—hard to explain. I can look into a person's mind and their history, and I can see strings into other timelines and other people and beliefs. It unfolds as I get more connected to the person in the healing. At first it might be a small image or feeling, but as I pull on it, I can see more of a tapestry of life inside his or her mind, or thought, or inside their being. I can actually see the bodies that surround the person while I'm working on them. My friend Abby Wheat was the best at this of anyone I've met so far. Her ability to clear energy and 'strings' was so powerful.

She said she would come to the last channeling. You'll like her. She is pure angel, which means third dimension is also tough for her."

Sarabeth smiles at Lance.

"I used to love working on you in fifth. I learned so much about your angel you in that space: I called that your fifth Lance. It really helped me help you here in this dimension. It helped me see your true self. Fifth Lance, that freer, more spiritually aligned you, collaborated with me to bring into your third-dimensional consciousness who you really are. It was powerful. You are quite a being, my love."

Sophia and Rob run in.

"Hi, guys, what are you doing?" Rob says, leaning in and kissing Sarabeth's cheek. "I think we need to feed everyone."

"What are we eating tonight, Mom? Are you going to make us dinner, Lance? I love your dinners."

Sophia squeezes in on the chair in between Sarabeth and Lance. Lance puts his hand on Sophia's shoulder.

"Well, I will if you help me. What do you say?"

"Yes. Yes."

Sophia jumps up and goes over to the refrigerator. Rob and Sarabeth walk out of the kitchen together.

"Have fun you two," Sarabeth calls back at them.

Sarabeth leans in toward Rob.

"How are you doing with all of that information from the channel?"

Rob walks quietly next to Sarabeth.

"I want to talk with you about Lance."

They walk into the study upstairs.

"I don't like him here. It brings up everything that happened years ago. And then the channel communicating how I owe him my life from past timelines, and you and him corded for this this timeline. I don't know what to do. This is outside my comfort space. I'm just a painter."

Rob removes his glasses and rubs his eyes. His strawberry blonde hair goes in all directions.

Sarabeth walks over to him and sits down on the couch. Rob looks up at her as her long brown hair is falling into her face. She pushes it aside.

"Before you knew about me and Lance, you and Lance seemed to have a connection, too. I mean in third dimension. He said you shared so much with him. You must have felt this connection the channel was talking about."

"Yeah, I did. But it is so confusing. I don't want to lose you. When I see Sophia with him it is worse than when I think of you and him together. I don't understand how you navigate these dimensions, these feelings inside you. It seems impossible for me to make the best decision, to let go and trust this untouchable time and space dimension."

"It isn't easy for me either. I love you both. I know that's hard to hear, but it's extraordinarily difficult for me, even with my deep connection to the dimensions. I'm trying to discern what is best for us and align us to our heart connection and time and space. I don't know what to do either, but I am worried about you, Rob."

Lance and Sophia are laughing in the kitchen.

"Lance, how come you and my dad never talk to each other?

Lance closes his eyes and turns over the chicken in the skillet. He replaces the skillet into the oven and looks over at Sophia, who's sitting on the counter.

"Hey, I thought you aren't supposed to sit on the counter."

Sophia slides down off the counter and sits in the chair.

"Are you ignoring my question?"

Lance sets the timer and sits down next to Sophia.

"No, I'm not. It's complicated Sophia, your dad's and my relationship. I think he is mad at me."

"But didn't the channel say you and he were like brothers?

"Yes, that's true, but sometimes brothers get angry with each other and they have to take time to get through that anger. I think your dad just needs more time."

Sophia looks at Lance and she puts her hand on his shoulder.

"It makes me sad. You look so sad too, but I see something else in your eyes, I can't tell, it's like you look guilty. Did you do something wrong to make my dad so mad?"

"Yeah, I did and I didn't. It's hard to explain. But yes, I do feel guilty. I think—"

The buzzer goes off on the stove. Lance gets up, grabs the potholder and takes out the skillet.

"Let's talk more about it later, Sophia, OK?"

"OK, Lance. I hope you and my dad work it out. Maybe you should apologize for what you did? That's what Mom says to do when I feel like I made a mistake."

Lance smiles.

"Yeah, that's good advice, Sophia. Let's get the rest of this dinner ready for everyone. Where does your mom keep the serving stuff? Is it up here?"

Sophia pulls over a chair and reaches to the cabinet above the espresso machine.

"It's up here."

Together they pull down the dishes.

Peter enters the kitchen.

"Hi, are we eating soon?"

Sophia turns around. Lance keeps dishing the food into the dish.

"Hi, Peter!" They both say, and then start laughing.

"Yeah, I think it will be ready in about 10 minutes. Will you get everyone? Sophia, you help him, OK?"

CHAPTER 12

Life in harmony is a process of continual transformation.
—Taoist principle

Psyche, butterfly, breath of life, breeze—life giving wind; the energy of heaven and earth, divinity and humanity, spiritual energies and the physical matrix of the body.
—Ancient Greek philosophy

The five spirits are the Taoist map of the human psyche. The system provides a mythical view of the nervous system. The five spirits can be understood as the Taoist view of the chakra system of Vedic India. The spirits exist as centers of consciousness in the subtle body and vibrate to a particular consciousness and a particular vibration or frequency of psychic energy. These are the key, which opens the doorway to the mysteries of the Taoist psycho-spiritual alchemy.
—Lorie Eve Decher, The 5 Spirits

Sarabeth is walking in a large labyrinth. It is green all around her. The smell of citrus fills her. She feels slightly anxious as she follows the path. As she focuses on the birds and rustling of the leaves, her heart slows. In the background she hears crows cawing. She smiles at their playfulness. She feels the urgency of completing her test. She sees her feet in light sandals, with white fabric flowing around her ankles. She is hurrying to complete the labyrinth without getting lost in the interior dead ends.

Facing a tall wall of green, she closes her eyes and meditates, lightly asking her inner guide which way to go. She feels a gentle pull of energy to her left and turns in that direction. She sees a butterfly ahead of her. She is drawn to follow the butterfly. Within moments, the space opens up, and she sees Lance standing at the center, staring at the family pomegranate tree bursting with fruit; a butterfly lands on the branch closest to her.

As she reaches toward the branch, the butterfly lifts off and lightly lands in her hand. The wings are yellow and black with intense blue, the color of a swallowtail. She waits for a message, her heart beating fast in her chest. Focusing on the gentle movement of the butterfly wings, she slows her heartbeat. She breathes in and out, keeping focus on the fruit on the tree in front of her: bright red pomegranates bursting with color and life. She breathes; pomegranate and butterfly, psyche and Pandora's box, Persephone and Demeter, what's the connection? She breathes and opens her mind as she searches for connections, the cycle of life and death, transformation, the subconscious, the depth of yin, the underworld, the void, Mary Magdalene and the alabaster jar. She feels Lance's presence close to her. This must be about the importance of balancing masculine with the divine feminine.

The garden is moving away; Sarabeth is lightly floating in space. Stars spin by. She gently slows at different constellations to view, as if they are familiar friends. The stars stop moving; she floats down to a space of white rocks in the shape of a labyrinth with one path to the center. Waves of water crash about her. Sarabeth moves through the labyrinth as if flying, floating 18 inches off the ground. The scent of olive trees energize her. She floats down to the center, a stone slab with a group of white flowers and seashells set atop it.

She is home and he is there. Her heart swells with joy. Sarabeth again sees a white cloth around her ankles, this time with a gold trim and flat sandals that tie around her ankles. Next to the shells is a filled ceramic wine goblet etched with the shape of a butterfly, a double-sided Labrys ax, and a potted olive tree. Sarabeth greets Lance with a kiss, takes a drink from the glass, and speaks a prayer in ancient Greek. She dances back toward the entrance. She stops halfway and returns. She sees an image of Ariadne. She breathes and waits for a message. Her vision is filled with women dancing in robes that only *cover their hips; she witnesses a whole culture of sacred action with women as the leaders.*

The white stones are moving away; Sarabeth is lightly floating in space, stars spinning by. The stars stop moving; she floats down to a mound of brown rocks on brown dirt placed in the shape of a labyrinth with a single path to the center. Flutes and drums play in the background as she dances in moccasins through the labyrinth. At the center sit feathers and corn on a low brown mound of dirt. The smell of burning sage and cedar rises from branches stuck into the dirt. It fills her with a sense of peace. From behind the mound Sarabeth sees another dancer, a man. Returning the cedar branch to the mound, Sarabeth sets out after him. Just as she meets up with him, as he turns his face toward her, she sees Lance. They embrace.

Sarabeth wakes with a start. She still feels the images and energy of her dream. She grabs her notebook on the table next to her and gently leaves her bed. She sits on her couch in her study. She writes down the new information from her dream. The sun rising from behind the mountain outside her window colors her room pink and orange. She sets down the book, stretches out on her couch, and closes her eyes.

Sophia is in the alcove watching Liu Ruyi. The smell of jasmine lightens her fears. On his desk are many pages of writings. Sophia can see some of the pages and recognizes the words. Liu Ruyi is drinking tea. He stops to talk with a man. Sophia recognizes it's his father warning him. Sophia longs to go closer to the men but is afraid of being seen. From the alcove she reads the top pages on Liu Ruyi's writing table: "Energy alchemy formula."

The older man is talking about a serious matter; his voice has dropped almost to a whisper. He is speaking in a dialect of Chinese, but the words are translated in Sophia's mind.

"You must be careful; she is set on taking your life. She sees you as an impediment to her son's transition to emperor. It is serious! You must give your manuscript to someone you trust so that the

information won't be lost. She plans to destroy it, and you. She has a great deal of power among the advisers."

Sophia watches as Liu Ruyi sips his tea. He does not appear to be upset by the conversation. Sophia feels a deep love and pride toward Liu Ruyi rising within her being. Now Liu Ruyi is talking. Again he speaks in a Chinese dialect that is completely understandable to Sophia as she watches.

"I must do my work. If she must destroy me, then she must; I cannot hide or be something I am not. I can only do my work and create this important document for the good of all. If she takes it, there will be another who comes and brings forth the information."

Liu Ruyi pauses and looks toward the alcove with an almost imperceptible nod toward Sophia, then he continues as if speaking directly to Sophia.

"It is not my knowledge—I am only an interpreter of the information to bring it forth. If the time continuum shifts and this is not the time, another will come. I know this. We must allow the energies to flow with the guidance of the people. We cannot go against the flow of things; we cannot go against the Tao. It is. We are a part of it, not the directors of it."

Liu Ruyi sips his tea and looks directly at the old man.

"You are my benefactor and my friend. I am deeply grateful to you for your love and guidance, and your friendship. If the time comes and I am killed, do not grieve my loss. Celebrate our time together and our deep understanding of each other and our work. Be at peace regardless of the outcome; all is as it should be."

He hands his friend some tea and nods lightly at him. They leave together. The pages are on Liu Ruyi's desk. Sophia goes into the room. As she stands over the table, she reads the energy alchemy formula. She realizes the simplicity of it and identifies several characters to assist her in remembering it. Hearing Liu Ruyi returning, she bolts back into the alcove just as he enters the room.

Sophia awakes with intensified energy. The information is still in her mind from the dream. Sophia feels a deep sadness about her friend, yet an urgency to write. She jumps out of her bed and walks down the hall to her father's studio. As she passes her parents' room she sees her mom in her study lying on the couch. The sun is filtering into her room. Sophia goes into her father's studio, trying to be quiet and not wake Lance. She picks up her journal and special paints, goes over to her father's desk, and begins to write down what she saw in Liu Ruyi's papers. She can still translate some of the Chinese letters and the images from the formula. With each passing minute she loses more of the material from her memory. She writes furiously. After a while she puts down the pen and lays her head on the desk on top of the images she has replicated. She can hear people in the kitchen. She falls back into a deep sleep.

Sophia is in the alcove again, watching Liu Ruyi. She smells the jasmine and sees his desk. The pages of writings are gone. Liu Ruyi is in the room. His head on the desk and his robe is falling down onto the chair. Sophia feels danger. She leaves the alcove; furtively checking for others in the room, she goes to Liu Ruyi. His eyes are closed.

"Liu Ruyi, are you OK?"

He opens his eyes.

"It is the end. Do not worry; you will bring forth the information. I trust in you."

Sophia, now crying, touches Liu Ruyi's hand.

"But how will I know?"

"I hid a copy in there," he says, pointing to a drawer in his desk. "Take it. Go. They will return quickly and search my room."

Sophia takes the papers from the desk and returns to the alcove, just as she hears footsteps in the hallway.

She awakens to find Lance gently touching her shoulder.

"Sophia, are you OK? You seem to be having a bad dream."

Sophia sits up and looks around, slightly dazed.

"I was, Lance, I was having a bad dream. It was horrible."

She leans into him.

"It was Liu Ruyi. He was dying. But he gave me the writings. I took them from where he had hidden them. I mean, I took them in the dream. I've been trying to remember what they said so I can show Mom and Peter and Jan. They'll know what it all means."

Lance holds Sophia.

"Do you want me to get your mom?"

Sophia puts her arms around Lance, hiding her face in his chest.

"No, it's good you are here. I feel safe with you."

Just then Sarabeth walks into the studio.

"Sophia, Lance, what's going on? Are you OK, Sophia?"

"Mom, come here. I want you to look at what I wrote down from my dream. It's the lost information from Liu Ruyi."

Sophia is pulling the papers together with the images she's drawn and hands them to Sarabeth.

"Look Mom, see? I tried to remember everything."

Sarabeth takes the pages.

"Sophia, this is very powerful information. The pictures are so clear and descriptive. You have done such a fine job relaying it. It's like what the ancient Taoists wrote about how the brain and nervous system interact with the five spirits to maintain health and balance. This is amazing, dear. We have to show it to Peter. Let's go downstairs."

Sarabeth leaves the room quickly, papers in hand. Lance reaches over to Sophia.

"Do you want me to go with you downstairs?

"Yes please, Lance. I'm so tired and I still feel sad about my dream."

Sophia takes Lance's hand.

"OK, I'm ready. Let's go."

Sarabeth bounds down the stairs toward the kitchen. She is greeted by the sounds of Peter, Bob, and Debbie excitedly chatting.

"Peter, look," she says, holding out Sophia's drawings and notes from her dream. "Sophia had another dream; this time she was able to decipher the Chinese lettering while still in the dream state. It's phenomenal. It's just like the Taoist concept of how the five spirits are the map of the human psyche. It shows the same points that are like whorls of energy for the five spirits. Do you see what I mean?"

Peter takes the papers and looks through them, studying the drawings.

"Sarabeth, how could she have seen this so clearly? This is extraordinary."

Debbie and Bob step over from the other side of the counter to look at the drawings. Debbie looks at Sophia as she walks down the stairs, leaning into Lance.

"This is a very powerful dream that you had, young lady."

Sophia leans farther into Lance. "It made me so sad, Debbie. Liu Ruyi died; but before he did he said that he knew I would bring this knowledge forth. He was so sweet and gentle and strong! I'm a little nervous about it all."

Rob glances at the monitor in the south side of the kitchen.

"Sarabeth, I see Abby coming up the path." He points to the camera as she passes out of frame.

"OK, I'll go let her in." Sarabeth turns to Peter. "Hey, I'm going to have her stay in the den. Can you and Jan do yoga on the front patio tomorrow morning?"

"Yes, sure we can. No problem." Peter turns to Sophia. "Let's go out back to work on this."

"OK, that sounds great, Peter." She leaves Lance's side and gathers all her notes and drawings. "Let's go!"

At the door, Abby waits, her long blonde hair tied into a messy bun. Dressed in yoga attire, her tiny frame wears the clothes loosely. Sarabeth greets her with a smile.

"I'm so glad to see you, Abby. Come in. There's a lot going on. Let me catch you up."

They walk toward the den. Inside the room, Abby smiles and hugs Sarabeth.

"Hey, I got such a heavy slime feeling as soon as I came into the house. What's going on?"

Abby sits down on the blue leather couch in the den. Sarabeth sits next to her.

"Huh, I don't know. I mean, there is a lot happening with Lance and Rob and me. The channel shared so much information about the past timelines. It's really pulling on all three of us. Is that what you're feeling?"

"No, it feels more ominous, like something bad is going to happen. I started to feel it as I drove onto the property."

"Well, there's been a lot of energy, an amazing high frequency of light. And Sophia has been dreaming of a death. Do you think that's it? They're working on the dream out back."

"It's something else."

Abby closes her eyes and feels within, checking to see what comes to her.

"Sarabeth, it feels like someone is going to die. It feels so strong, so intense."

Abby's body shakes.

Sarabeth hears Laurel in the hallway.

"Bob, have you seen Sarabeth? I have to talk with her."

Sarabeth turns to Abby.

"I'm going to see what she wants. This is where I have you staying; the kitchen is just across the hall and there is a bathroom just next to it in the hallway. OK?"

Abby hugs her again.

Sarabeth calls out to Laurel. "Hey, I'm in here, Laurel. Just a sec, I'll be right there."

They meet in the hall. "Hey, what's up? You sound worried. Is everything OK with you and Debbie?"

"Yes—that's not it. I keep feeling something. Walk to my room with me, OK?"

Sarabeth and Laurel walk to the room at the end of the hall. Once inside Laurel turns to Sarabeth.

"I have a really bad feeling, Sar. At first I thought I was just picking up on Rob's pain about what the channel said and Lance's energy with you. But it's more than that. Something really dark is coming in, like it's palpable. Have you been feeling it?"

Sarabeth falls into the chair by the desk.

"No, I haven't. Abby just said the same thing though. She said she felt it when she came into the house. Usually it just knocks me over, but I don't feel anything. I'll go upstairs and meditate. I can't understand what is going on. Do you want to check in with Abby? She's very sensitive like you— well, it's different from you, she doesn't see ghosts so much as she can feel the energy. She's very sensitive. Come on, I'll introduce you."

Sarabeth shakes her head.

"Laurel, that information that came through, I'm worried that Rob didn't take it well. He told me he is really upset. But it's not just emotional: I could see in his eyes, it disrupted him. It's like the light in them is covered over with this flatness. He doesn't deal in these different dimensions. It's like all his cells were blown apart inside him. I'm worried he isn't thinking clearly."

"Maybe if Abby and I talk we can figure it out. We can go into fifth and work on it together."

Laurel and Sarabeth walk down the hallway. Abby is sitting on the couch in the den.

"Hi, Abby, this is Laurel. She is feeling the same thing as you. I think maybe you gals can see what you can find out together in fifth."

Sarabeth leaves and walks directly upstairs to her study. She notices the door to Rob's studio is closed. She thinks,

That's weird. I wonder if it's Rob or Lance in there. She sees Leo in her room and immediately feels more peaceful. "Hi there, boy," she says, petting his head.

In the study, Rob is sitting at the desk. His thoughts are racing: *Everything feels so messed up. I can't seem to get a handle on this whole thing.* He sees flashes of when he first found Lance and Sarabeth together, her hair flowing down her back as she embraces Lance, his legs and arms holding her. He shakes his head to make the image leave. Anger and rage fill his chest.

Laurel and Abby are on the front porch. Abby places crystals she brought with her on Laurel's body in a grid.

"How is this going to help?" Laurel asks.

Abby is listening to the angels direct her. She pauses to respond.

"Oh, the angels are telling me how to place them. Once done, I can feel into your energy to see what is going on. You are somehow connected to the energy. This will give us a way in to see what it is and if we can shift it. It's like a portal into the higher dimensions."

"Oh, OK. What do you want me to do?"

"It will open a portal. You will be able to see. Together we will work to shift it."

"Oh. Now I remember Sarabeth telling me about your work together. OK, I'm ready."

Abby closes her eyes and is directed to work at Laurel's occiput. Immediately she sees images of a battle: two men fighting, dressed as knights in armor. A woman is there but not in the battle. She has long blonde hair. Then she sees two men again fighting in costumes she doesn't recognize. Their hair is long and black, and the clothing is bright blue; a woman also with long black hair is present, but not fighting. The energy is that she is the cause of the battle. There are threads connecting to two men at the conference. She can't quite make out their physical features. She asks her guides what is happening and what to do. She is directed to pull out threads from the third eye, solar plexus, and sacral chakras. As she does this, she hears Laurel.

"Abby, I feel like I need to throw up. I have to get up. Is that OK? My stomach is really in pain. Is it something you're doing?"

"I don't know. Just give me a few more minutes. I'm almost finished."

Abby focuses her energy on Laurel's solar plexus. She takes a black lava stone shaped like an egg from her bag of stones and presses it in on her solar plexus. She sees a ball of strings connected there and into her mind. She continues pressing on that space. She feels the ball coming into the stone, a "sucker" stone she calls it, and smiles to herself. As she pulls out the ball she hears this is karmic—even if you pull out the strings it may still happen. Then she sees the images again. Each time one of the men is limp, blood coming out of him. The image shocks her and she pulls out of the meditation.

"Abby, are you OK? What happened?" Laurel asks. She feels dizzy, but the nausea is gone.

"Yeah, I'm OK. I just got scared and it pulled me out of the work. Are you OK?"

Laurel slowly sits up. She moves the stones off of her. "I don't feel sick anymore but I am dizzy."

"You may have come out too quickly. Take a few breaths in and out. Is that better?"

Abby is standing close to Laurel, her tiny frame belies her immense power.

"I saw two men in different clothing fighting to the death. Then I saw they are connected to two men here, but I didn't recognize them. I don't know anyone here except Sarabeth and Sophia. I tried to shift the energy, but they stopped me. I think something is going to happen soon."

Laurel sits up.

"Do you mean someone is going to kill someone here at the retreat? Oh no. We have to tell Sarabeth."

Peter, Bob, Debbie, and Sophia are on the back patio. Jan walks out to join them.

"What are you all doing?"

Peter motions for Jan to come over to him. "Look at what Sophia dreamed."

Jan picks up the drawings in amazement. "But how did she know this? Was it Liu Ruyi? This is extraordinary. It is actually showing more than what we know from our studies, Peter."

"I know."

Debbie asks, "So why do you think this is coming through now, here? And how can we use this in our work?"

Peter shakes his head. "I'm not sure. I think it has something to do with what the channel said but I don't fully understand the significance of it yet. What do you think, Jan?"

Jan is looking over all the images. "Peter, it's showing something we haven't seen before: something feminine. The way it's being presented is less like the mountain that we have always read about in our studies—it's more like a spiral or a labyrinth. Do you see that here? Look!"

Peter looks at the pages. He looks up at Jan. "I see what you mean." He looks at Bob. "Do you remember what Rob said the other day when he was drawing, about Sarabeth's dreams? She was dreaming of herself going through labyrinths in different cultures."

Bob takes off his glasses and takes the pages from Peter. After a while he looks at Peter. "This is what we have been missing, the divine feminine." He plants his gaze upon Debbie. "What is the meaning of dreaming of a labyrinth in Jungian theory? I can't remember. Isn't it from an old culture, something to do with goddess worship?"

"Yes, myths about labyrinths are thousands of years old. Some say it dates back to a spiritual religion or culture that had to do with goddess worship, where the concepts of source were masculine and feminine, like how we view the yin-yang symbol. I remember images of it in Jung's *The Red Book*. The center items are typically feminine symbols. It is seen both as a way to reconnect with the inner feminine, but in dreaming of a labyrinth it is about the subconscious—a spiritual journey to the center of your soul. Did Rob say what she saw there? That matters. It generally tells her what her soul path and subconscious dilemma is, and it connects her to her spiritual path. This means at the same time that Liu Ruyi was offering this information to Sophia, Sarabeth was receiving energy and information about how to use it, and the channel has been giving us related tools also. This is extraordinary, the tapestry of it all. Jung would say it is synchronicity."

Debbie places the pages on the table, pushes her thick blond hair back with her glasses, and sits down. She stares off toward the dig.

Jan turns to Peter. "So, the five spirits open the way to one's spiritual path to overcome the base secondary nature and choose or awaken the spiritual path. Using it like a mountain doesn't allow for that inner process or the aspect of the divine feminine."

Peter nods. "I wonder what was in the center of Sarabeth's dream labyrinths? Sophia, did your mom tell you?"

Sophia shakes her head. "No, I was so focused on my dream, she didn't talk with me about it."

Sarabeth is deep in meditation in her study. She feels off. Her head hurts as if she has a migraine. She knows this indicates she is resisting information from the channel. She breathes in and out three times. Breathing deeply, she centers on her fourth chakra in the center of her chest filling it with light. She brings her attention to the chakra 18 inches above her head. She sees light pouring into it and she shifts it to golden light at six inches above her head. As she concentrates with an open heart, she feels her headaches lift. She grounds her bare feet onto the floor under her couch, imagining roots diving deep into the earth, and wraps them around her earth chakra.

Immediately she is shown two men battling in knights clothing: one dark-haired, one light-blond-haired. The battle intensifies. She feels her heart breaking as the dark-haired man holds the knife above the blond man's chest. As it drives down, she sees it stick firmly into the ground. The blond man says, "You will have to kill me, or I will kill you." The dark-haired man steps away. "I won't kill you. I can't. You are my brother. I will leave. Take care of her for me. She deserves care." Sarabeth's heart is beating so rapidly she feels dizzy. She breathes three times and waits for more images to appear. She only sees darkness. A tiny image begins to appear in the center of the darkness: It is a flaming, colorful depiction of Metatron's cube. It fills her inner vision, as if it is coming toward her. Suddenly, she feels it hit her physical body and surround her. She feels completely calm and at peace, protected.

Sarabeth opens her eyes. The sun is setting. Her room is ablaze with golden orange and yellow light. She stretches out her hand to pet Leo at her feet and grabs the palo santo on her table. She lights it and smudges herself.

Rob enters the room.

"Hi, Sara, it's time."

Sarabeth turns to face Rob,

"OK. Hey, are you alright? I saw your door was closed when I came up. You never do that."

"Yeah, I needed some privacy. Let's go downstairs for tonight's channeling."

When Rob and Sarabeth enter the room they see that everyone has preceded them. Laurel and Abby are sitting together on the back couch. Rob takes the open chair farthest from Lance.

Sarabeth sits down on the white couch facing her friends. "It's so nice to see such a big group. Abby Wheat has joined us in the back near Laurel. She will have an opportunity to share her experiences with us after the channeling. I asked her to come because she works in the higher dimensions, and I think the channel will want to reference her work tonight."

Abby smiles and waves at everyone. "Hi."

"There is a lot of electricity in the air tonight. Let's each take a few breaths and focus our energy to connect to source."

Sarabeth sits in a relaxed position, imagining light coming in the top of her head and moving down through her spine. She remembers the image of Metatron's cube and relaxes. She opens her eyes and sees her friends surrounded in light. She looks at Rob and sees his energy is slightly chaotic; she sends light to him.

Sarabeth puts a lozenge into her mouth and takes another deep, cleansing breath as she begins her inner directing mantra. "OK, let's begin:

"*Source energy, allow me to be a clear healing channel. I call in one hundred thousand angels to please come in and fill this room; I invite in only high frequency light beings. Please come in to guide me and offer me interpretation for this sixth evening of this retreat on healing psycho-emotional trauma through the ancient traditions... Thank you for your protection and guidance dear Archangel Michael, the Council of Twelve, Archangel Raphael, Mercury, Metatron, the Marys, Orion, and Sirius.*"

Sarabeth relaxes into her chair, feeling a deep love overwhelming her. She feels the voice and words from the channel. Her voice lightens and softens as she speaks the words, augmented by the complete knowing of what is being shared.

"*Dearly beloved, we are here for the sixth night of this invaluable retreat, and we want you to know how much we love each of you. It is a joy to assist you in bringing increased light into your vessels as you choose to have this experience. Intention and attention in a light yet clarified way assists you to open further to your healing capacity and to receive the historical traditions you desire. Through this process you discover more fully how all is energy and light.*

"We are grateful for your ongoing focus and attention to the light and the ancient knowledge found within. Integration of spirit, mind, and body are necessary for healing and health. To increase your integration process, experience a sense of allowing. To be at peace within, go into your heart center and open to love. From an open heart center you are able to receive a higher frequency of light. Anchor this in your field through intention and connection to source; you may imagine this as a light that moves through your chakra system and anchors into your field. Think of this as if you are stepping into the light, and the light pours in through and around you.

"Remember that attention and intention focus energy and creation...you create that to which you put your attention. Pay attention to that which brings you joy, that which you desire, and this is what you will create. You choose your creation through your attention and intention and the energy of love. Love promotes the blossoming of life; fear condenses and constricts. Fear cannot exist where there is love. To open to love, take in a deep breath and fill your lungs. As you exhale, feel the air moving through your body. Focus your attention on your heart space as you feel the pulsing there and the exchange of air in your lungs. Open your mind. Drop your attention from your thinking to your heart space. It is your feeling, but it is feeling informed by compassion and a sense of security in love. Come from your heart space and you will be in the energy of love, in the space of love. This energy allows for direct communication with spirit, compassion, and light.

"The energies of flow and allowing are key to increasing the frequency of light. Allowing each emotion its expression, with love and compassion, allows for it to be released and you to be guided to your true essential being. From this space you can see what is in your best interest, and out of a natural inner guidance, be guided by what brings you joy. The continuum of control and allowing is connected to creation and ownership in your life path.

"We discussed in previous channelings the importance of whole foods, fresh water, movement, daily meditation, and clean air, breath. And that both excess and insufficiency create dissonance in the balance within, dull the capacity for light, and lead to disease within each person.

"Today's interpretation is on how to incorporate the knowledge from your intuition and various timelines into your soul path. We see that this is most useful with respect to relationship, friendships, partnerships, and love relationships.

"Last night we spoke about how each soul has a relationship to a group, and often comes into incarnation with a set of agreements to fulfill. This is a layered process and includes what is called 'karma,' or karmic agreements. Most, but not all, of what drives a spirit-human are these soul agreements made prior to incarnation. There are different timeline dimensions and there are relationships from past and future lives that affect what choices a being makes throughout her life. This is at its core driven by the soul purpose of each spirit human.

Each being may have some conscious knowledge of the agreements driving his or her decisions—or not. This is driven by the being's soul. The level at which she is connected to her soul agreements indicates the level of conscious awareness regarding these decisions. In some circumstances, one being may have more knowing than another and this can create pain.

Time is not what you think it is. It is not linear. We speak of it that way to conform to your perspective of it in the third dimension. The fourth dimension is the space from which karma arises. Once you get into the fifth dimension you see that spirit is the powerful creator. You are made up of the tapestry of your and your ancestors' lives—it is woven in what you think of as your DNA. For many of you, access to this is blocked in a cognitive way. It directs you through emotion, your senses, what you feel as something subtle driving you toward a relationship or connection.

We spoke in a previous channeling about the fifth dimension of consciousness. And the difference between intuition and ego-based drives in terms of how you experience them. Like the issue of attention and intention, your work is to assist yourself and others to focus on the intuition and release the ego-based drives. This appears to be difficult for humans, as the thing you need to release feels more intense and the thing you need to focus on is subtle. Living in third intensity 'feels' like the thing to focus on, and as so often happens as one is elevating the consciousness, one gets stuck in an intense cycle of patterning. We spoke of using your heart center to help jump you out of that rut, as well as acupuncture points and other tools to help realign you to balance so you can hear and listen to that inner soul voice.

"You each have fifth-dimensional selves assisting you. Begin in this dimension to see time as all happening simultaneously. The future and past have a spiraling quality to them. You can see these aspects of yourselves as your high self: the soul overlay who is still connected to your soul group and who comes from a space of pure love and exists directly connected to source. You can access your fifth-dimensional self via meditation.

"Working in fifth is one of the most powerful ways to access source and create health, turning back disease to the proper flow of energy. Sarabeth and her friend Abby Wheat have been doing this work for several years now. To understand the power of the fifth dimension of healing you have to be willing to accept that alignment with spirit and your spiritual path is a direct connection to source. You must let go of your mind being in control and be at peace with the concept of one source of light. The part that usually blocks this is attachment to mind, and the illusion of control, and the personality you call the ego.

"Let's discuss timelines again. Time is all happening at once. It is like string theory from physics: many happenings at the same time. The being has the ability to comprehend between one and five happenings at a time. So, for those stuck in third dimension, the idea of birth and death and linear time is the only possible perception. As one opens to this idea, there are possibilities of past lives and future lives along the linear continuum.

"The spirit-human evolution is happening multidimensionally. This shift is ramping up and moving at a faster pace over the last year, and this will continue to take on speed. The metaphor of the labyrinth is the way in which we want you to consider your way through to evolution of your consciousness and that of your clients. To move through the labyrinth efficiently you need access to that quiet voice. The way this applies to your consciousness is how you have to develop your internal connection to your soul and listen to the subtle sensations and intuitions as you are interacting with others in relationship. Fear and ego-based drives can interfere with this.

Begin to experience a deep connection with source in your everyday lives, bringing your connection and fifth-dimensional experiences into your everyday practices and lives. Focus on holding a connection to the divine feminine within you. You can connect this through a direct connection with that aspect of the divine if you are already living in sixth or seventh dimension, as some of you are, or by way of connecting to an archetype who holds that nature, White Buffalo Woman, white or green Tara, Quan Yin, Mary, Shekinah, Mary Magdalene, Lady Nada, are some ascended masters or archetypes that hold this high-level divine feminine energy. Earlier interpretations discussed that balance of yin with yang or masculine and feminine to be the pivot point of the Tao. All these offerings are leading you toward balance or right action to remain on your soul path.

"There is so much to share on this subject of soul connections, karma, and timelines, and the labyrinth as a model for inner-directed enlightenment that leads you to your soul connection and soul path and the elevation of consciousness. We are aware that you have questions and would like to answer these to your completion. Several of us have spoken in this time, and many high light beings are ready to provide loving guidance and information for you. We want you to know how much we love you and how grateful we are to be your interpreters for this information.

"We are available for specific questions...remember to drink plenty of water to assist your assimilation of this information at the cellular level as you are integrating this information and increasing the degree and frequency of light you are each holding; today it may be best to cleanse your energy field with asafetida and frankincense as

well as salt; and allow yourselves plenty of rest to help with assimila-
tion of this information. Grounding foods will be essential. You may
ground by walking on the earth or grass in your bare feet. Salt on the
balls of your feet will assist to bring you into your bodies while simul-
taneously encouraging the anchoring of the light and new information.

"There is another thing we want to share with you, Rob. We
see that you are suffering from the earlier interpretation. We want
you to know there is only love and you are deeply loved, and your
soul path is accessible to you if you can allay your deep fears and
anger. Know that Archangel Haniel is with you to help with your
confusion and pain. Your freedom comes from jumping over that
rut through self-love and trust. Your soul path is beautiful—please
open yourself to it. We understand how these karmic agreements,
which are at cross-purposes in this lifetime, make you unsure as
to what is the best thing to do. We encourage you to act from your
soul center toward its highest goal. This is an example of where
the secondary drives of the personality can interfere with the soul
guidance. Finding peace will require you facing your fears and
moving to divine love and forgiveness. We offer this information
with the highest love and light.

"We are so pleased to have this opportunity to share this infor-
mation and love you very much...we await your questions."

Sarabeth lightly speaks.

"Thank you so much The Pleiadians, Mercury, the
Council of Twelve, Archangel Uriel, Orion, the Marys,
Archangel Ariel, Archangel Raphael, Archangel Gabriel,
and Metatron. I am so grateful for this information. Please,
whoever is ready, you may ask your questions."

Sarabeth opens her eyes and looks lovingly at Rob. She
sees his energy is knotted and tight. She smiles at him with
compassion.

Jan says, "I do. May I proceed?"

"Yes, please go ahead." Sarabeth smiles at her friend.

"Sophia has this amazing dream and connection with
Liu Ruyi, and we have all been looking at the information,

and it seems that information is directly tied to this information on the divine feminine and labyrinths and healing. Are you going to talk about that?

"Hi, Jan. Yes, we will be talking about that tomorrow, and we will be channeling through Sophia for that offering. Can you wait until then to receive the information?"

Jan looks over at Sophia, who shrugs her shoulders, and says, "Yes, of course, but does that mean she already has the information now?"

"Yes and no. It is in her frequency but not in the conscious aspect of her mind that she has access to. We want to assist her in coming into her light frequency level by channeling through her the information that is already part of her soul. Is that OK with you, Sophia?"

Sophia looks at her mom and says, "Yes—it sounds scary and exciting!"

Abby asks, "Hey, is it OK if I ask a question, Sarabeth?"

Sarabeth opens her eyes and says, "Yes, of course. Please do."

"I want to understand how to maintain your connection in fifth and the higher dimensions and still manage the everyday issues of life in society. I seem to be able to be in the dimensions and work on my clients, but it seems I drop out completely when handling grocery shopping, childcare, and sometimes driving. You know, I get affected by outside influences and it's like I lose the connection. The experience is quite destabilizing."

"Welcome, Abby. We are very happy to see you here with this group. We have worked with you many times while you are in the higher dimensions and love your beautiful 'angel energy,' as Sarabeth calls it. This is an excellent question because it speaks to the most difficult aspect of being spirit-humans living on the planet at this time of transition into a higher level of consciousness. The process of daily living is, for the most part, a mind or ego state, yet the experience in the higher dimensions of consciousness becomes decreasingly individual.

Although you are following and connected to your soul path, you are also fantastically connected to all as one—especially in the upper dimensions ten through twelve. This means that at times you have to drop out of these to manage your physical life. We have noticed that when you are in fifth dimension this is less problematic for you. It allows for the deep connection to love and the webstrings between you and all things but also allows you to navigate third-dimensional and fourth-dimensional space. We have seen two effective ways to maintain this connection of fifth in third, as you call it.

First, maintain your physical, mental, and emotional bodies clear of debris such as misbeliefs, negative emotions, and low vibrational food. Second, imagine that surrounding your field is an egg of protection so that you can maintain the direct connection to source in your heart, with something like a spear or light cord that extends from your crown through your central chakras into the earth below. The egg of light or energy protection allows for the negative energy to bounce off and not get entangled into your causal body so that you can feel protected, connected, and open simultaneously.

You can use other geometric patterns like the flower of life, the merkaba, or Metatron's cube for increased protection and connection. Cleansing yourself with salt and baking soda between clients and after personal work and then sealing the energy field around you with flower water smudge and sound additionally helps. Does this answer your question"?

Abby opens her eyes, looks up and says, "Yes, that is very helpful. Thank you."

Sarabeth gently wipes tears from her eyes. "Thank you all high light beings for your support and your information today. You have offered so much today, thank you all. Archangel Michael, if you could clear the energy, thank you, thank you. Kadosh, kadosh, kadosh. Om, gam, Ganapataye, namaha. Om, shanti, shanti, shanti."

Sarabeth looks at her friends.

"How are you all doing? That was a very long reading and the information was more personally directed. This can be overwhelming. Take three cleansing breaths before you try to move around. As before, please remember to use whatever helpful grounding strategies you have discovered over the course of the last week before you go to sleep tonight."

Sarabeth notices that Rob has left the room. She motions for Lance to come over.

"Hey, did you notice when Rob left?"

"Yeah, it was after you went in to answer Abby's question. He didn't look good. Do you need me to help with anything?"

"No, I think I'll check in with Laurel and Abby and then get food ready in the kitchen. Are you OK just hanging out with Sophia for a bit?"

Lance smiles at Sarabeth.

"Of course. I would love that."

Lance walks over to Sophia "Hi. Do you want to show me the dig now?"

Sophia jumps up from her chair. "Yes. Let's go." Lance and Sophia walk out toward the front door.

Debbie, Jan, Bob, and Peter are huddled together in the middle of the room as Sarabeth passes them to greet Laurel and Abby. "Hi, you two. How was your work earlier? Did you figure out what you were feeling?

Abby looks at Laurel and then the others in the middle of the room. "Yeah, kind of. It wasn't a hundred percent clear, but definitely something bad is going to happen. We saw a lot of blood, and I heard it has a karmic connection. I tried to pull out the threads and shift the energy, but I still see something happening. It really scared me."

Laurel touches Abby's arm to comfort her.

"It really made me sick, Sarabeth. It was bad."

Sarabeth looks at her two friends. Her head is spinning. She is thinking about Rob and Lance and her guests. *What am I going to do?* she thinks to herself. *If Abby can't shift it, then I may not be able to either.* She turns her attention to the others.

"Hey, you guys, let's go get some food in the kitchen."

She turns to Abby.

"I made sure I have the food you like. Let's go in and ground. Maybe we can figure out what to do to avert this imminent event."

They all go into the kitchen.

CHAPTER 13

K o/Revolution (molting) Tui, the joyous, lake, above; Li, the clinging, fire, below. The judgment: revolution. On your own day you are believed. Supreme success, furthering through perseverance. Remorse disappears. (Revolutions are extremely grave matters, undertaken under duress of direct necessity...no other way out...only the man who has the confidence of the people, when the time is ripe, in the right way, so that he gladdens the people and by enlightening them prevents excesses...he must be free of selfish aims. Times change, seasons change, there is spring and autumn in the life of people, nations, and these call for social transformation.)

The image: Fire in the lake: the image of revolution. Thus the superior man sets the calendar in order and makes the seasons clear. Fire below and water above combat and destroy each other...so in the course of a year a combat takes place between the forces of light and darkness, eventuating in the revolution of the seasons...master these changes in nature by noting their regularity and marking off the passage of time accordingly...order and clarity appear in the apparently chaotic changes of the seasons...adjust in advance to the demands of the different times.

—The I Ching, #49, Ko/Revolution

Rob is pacing in his studio. Sarabeth walks in.

"Good morning, Rob. I didn't hear you get up. How are you this morning?"

She goes over to kiss him. He pulls away.

"Wait, Sarabeth. I'm not OK. I feel this electricity in me, like bees stinging me all over my body. I cannot sit or think. My nerves feel on fire."

He turns to her, walking away from his desk. She sees his 9mm handgun out on his desk.

"Rob, why is this out?

She goes over to it and checks the clip. Her heart sinks. Images of Laurel and Abby flash through her mind.

"Rob, it's loaded."

She releases the clip and the cartridge in the barrel. They fall onto the table. As she turns around, she feels Rob behind her.

"What are you doing?" he says. I need that."

He grabs the weapon from her and the clip off the table, and deftly rearms it. His beautiful blue eyes are black.

Sarabeth scans the room to calculate how to get to the door. She feels her heart in her ears. She realizes she is in danger. Rob is standing between her and the door. She looks toward the side balcony, but Rob's easel is blocking her way. As she steps into action, calm overwhelms her. She feels everything happening in slow motion, as if in a different dimension. Her senses are elevated, as if she can take in more information from all of them. She walks to the other side of the desk, picking up scissors on there as she passes them. She holds them tightly in her right hand at her side. Breathing deeply, she speaks in her calmest, most comforting voice.

"Rob, what do you need the gun for? Whatever you are going through, we can work it out. Take a breath."

"No, there is no way out," Rob yells. "I have to break this cycle. I can't do this again, what's happening with you and me and Lance. I can't."

He raises the gun and aims it toward Sarabeth.

Sarabeth continues to focus on calming Rob.

"Remember what the channel said: We can find peace. We just have to open our hearts and elevate our consciousness to those higher frequencies to find peaceful resolution. I love you. You love me. This is not the action you want to take. Feel your heart."

"That's all I feel. It's broken and on fire. I can't feel anything but that. Fuck the channel—every time I listen it's more about this."

Sarabeth feels her body tense up. She senses her words pushing him toward defiance rather than calm. She says in a quiet voice, "Rob, please, don't do this."

Lance is walking up the stairs with Sophia. He hears Rob yell, "I can't." He stops Sophia mid-step.

"Hey, Sophie, do you think you can go and see what Laurel and Abby are doing? I think I saw them on the front porch. Why don't you take them to the dig, OK?"

Sophia looks askance at Lance.

"But I thought we were going to do some drawing in Dad's study."

"Yeah, I know I said we would. But I just remembered I have to talk with a client on the phone. Is that OK if we do it in a little bit?"

"OK. I guess so."

Sophia turns and hops down the stairs yelling Laurel's name.

Lance watches to see her round the bottom of the stairs. As he sees her join Laurel and Abby he turns and runs up the stairs to the study. The door is closed. As he opens it, he sees Sarabeth to his left and Rob across the room aiming a gun at her. The energy in the room is electric, like the air before a thunderstorm. Reflexively, Lance lunges toward Rob, tackling him just as he fires. Sarabeth feels the bullet fly through her long, brown hair, tearing through her cheek as it passes. She drops the scissors and runs toward the door. Standing in the doorway, she feels herself pulled to the ground, like a dead weight unable to move. Out of the corner of her eye, through dripping blood, she sees them struggling in the corner of the room.

Why can't I move? she thinks to herself. Then she remembers what happened when her father died, as well as her friend Jen: How she was pulled to the ground as their soul connections left her. *No, NO! she screams in her mind. One of them is going to die.*

She hears the gun go off again and again. She sees them in a bundle on the floor, blood around them. Terrified for her life, she crawls out of the room, afraid that Rob will come after her. In her mind she calls out to Archangel Raphael to help her move. Then she feels herself lifted off the ground. She turns and sees Lance. He holds her.

"I have you, Beth. I have you. It's OK. I have you."

Sarabeth leans into his bloody chest.

"Is Rob OK? We need to call for help."

She gets up with Lance's help and walks to Rob's body. Blood drips out of an exit wound. She kneels next to him, brushing back his hair.

Lance steps over the body and sits next to her. "He's gone, Sarabeth. He doesn't have a pulse. Do you want to sit with him for a while?"

Sarabeth nods her head, quietly crying.

"Rob is the kindest man I know. His heart was so light, but there was this part of him that was always closed to spirit. I thought with the retreat he would find peace. He said he was struggling with us, what the channel said. I didn't understand how much it tortured him. It was like that part of him that was closed wouldn't let go of the pain."

Sarabeth is shaking. "When you came in, I was trying to find a way to get him back. I didn't see any way out of the room. His eyes were black. It was as if he was possessed. He wasn't making any sense."

Sarabeth shakes her head and looks down.

"If you hadn't come in, I would be the one lying in blood on the floor. Thank you, Lance, for saving me."

She holds him tightly for several minutes.

"How did you know to come in?" she eventually asks.

"I heard Rob's voice. There was something in it that sounded off. It felt like something really bad was happening. The hair on my neck was electric. Like static electricity in the air. He sounded on the edge. Sophia and I were halfway up the stairs when I stopped her and sent her to see Laurel. I suggested they go to the dig. I didn't want her anywhere near the study. I didn't know what was happening, but I could feel it was bad."

Peter, Bob, and Debbie are standing on the stairs looking at Lance and Sarabeth covered in blood.

"Sar, what happened?" Debbie asks, stepping toward Lance and Sarabeth. "We heard shots coming from up here. What is going on?"

Sarabeth leaves Lance and walks toward Debbie. Debbie takes her in her arms and hugs her.

"You're both bleeding. Lance, you look like you've been shot. Sar, where is Rob?"

Sarabeth starts to cry uncontrollably.

Bob and Peter pass Sarabeth and Debbie and walk toward the study door. Lance comes to the entryway and stops them. "You don't want to go in there. It isn't good. We need to call the police and the paramedics. I'm having a hard time breathing."

Peter looks at Lance. "You've been shot, Sarabeth's been shot, and Rob's been shot? What happened here?"

Bob dials 911 on his cell phone.

Lance motions the men toward him. "I came in and Rob was pointing a gun at Sarabeth. The energy in the room was chaotic. It was like I could feel the electrons in my cells spinning chaotically. It all happened so fast. I saw I had to act to save Sarabeth. I ducked under the line of fire and ran toward his chest. As I tackled him, the gun fired. It barely missed Sarabeth. It was the only way to protect her. We struggled. I was trying to get the gun from him but he was out of control. His eyes were black. The gun went off and the bullet went into my shoulder. He kept fighting me. It was like he was possessed, but just in the last minute I turned his hand around. I almost had the gun out of his hand when it went off again. He slumped down. I kicked the gun out of the way. I could see he wasn't moving so I checked his pulse. He was gone. Then I went to make sure Sarabeth was OK."

Peter looks at Lance and then through the study door, he sees Rob's body limp on the floor.

"Lance, this doesn't make any sense."

Peter is stunned. He shakes his head. He looks back at Lance's shoulder.

"We need to get some pressure on that wound. I'll get some towels from Sarabeth's room. I think you should wait here for the paramedics."

Peter starts to walk across the hall, then stops halfway.

"Bob, we need to keep Sophia away from here."

As he continues toward the bedroom, he thinks to himself, *Where is Jan?*

Lance leans against the wall as Bob holds the towel against his shoulder.

"Peter, before it happened, when I heard Rob yelling, I sent Sophia to be with Laurel and Abby. I think they went to the dig. But even if she didn't hear the shots, when she returns, she's going to come up here to look for me. You need to stop her. Can you and Jan take her somewhere away from here until after the police talk to Sarabeth and the paramedics treat her? Bob, can you and Debbie stay here with us to help with the police and paramedics?"

"Sure, of course we can stay and help," Bob says. "I called 911. They should be here soon."

Jan is talking with Laurel, Abby, and Sophia when she hears the sirens as they are entering the estate.

"Oh, my goodness," Jan says. "Why are they here? Do you think something happened?"

Laurel and Abby look at each other. Laurel takes Sophia's hand.

"Hey, let's go over to the far side of the dig and see what we can find."

"But shouldn't we see what that is about?" Sophia says.

Laurel smiles.

"No, I think we should go over here. Abby can join us in a minute."

Laurel and Sophia walk over to the far side of the dig. Abby looks at Jan.

"Jan, I can't go in there. I'm too sensitive. I can barely think even this far away. Can you go check? I'll stay here with Laurel and help her keep Sophia away until you come back, OK?"

Jan looks at Abby; her face is ashen.

"Abby, what is going on?"

Abby takes a deep breath.

"I'm not exactly sure. I had a premonition yesterday when I arrived. I could feel something bad was going to happen. I told Sarabeth about it. Then Laurel said she felt it too. We both tried to change the energy, working in fifth dimension. We saw two men battling. Laurel thinks it's Rob and Lance, because of something shared by the channel when I wasn't here. But it didn't seem to help. If its what we saw, I think it's heavy."

Jan stares at Abby.

"Abby, what did you feel when you had the premonition?"

"I felt someone was going to die. Laurel felt it too. She said she felt something ominous."

"OK, I'll go in and see how to help."

Jan starts to walk over to the house toward the flashing lights.

Sophia and Laurel are digging deep in the excavation site. As Laurel stands up, she sees Rob standing next to her. She knows that he is gone, and this is his ghost. She feels him communicating with her in her mind.

"*Can you tell Sophia how much I love her?*"

"*Rob, what happened?*"

"*I don't know. It was as if I was overtaken by this impulse that was so strong, I couldn't stop myself. I had to get out of this cycle between Sarabeth and Lance and me. Now that I'm here I understand what the channel was trying to avert with their words to me. But I couldn't make the leap. It was like all I could feel was anger, fear, and pain. Now I understand, but it's too late. Will you talk to her for me?*

"*I can't do it right now, Rob. I want to wait for Sarabeth to be with her.*"

Abby joins Sophia and Laurel.

"Laurel, are you OK?"

Laurel shifts her attention from Rob's ghost.

"Oh, yes I am. I was just thinking."

Laurel continues to see Rob's ghost next to Sophia. Unsure if Sophia can feel the energy, Laurel asks, "Hey Sophia, are you doing OK?"

"Yeah, it's just that all of a sudden I felt my dad. I wonder where he is. Do you think we should go back to find him?"

Abby hugs Sophia. "Not yet. Let's wait for your mom. What are you holding?"

Sophia shows Abby a broken flute. It has feathers tied to it. "Isn't it cool? I've never found anything like it before."

The police are finishing their work in the study. The main detective speaks to Sarabeth and Lance in the ambulance downstairs.

"I think it's clear what happened. We may have questions later though."

Sarabeth, still stunned, worries about how to complete the last day of the retreat.

"Can we go back in yet? I have guests here for a retreat. Is it OK if we continue?"

"Yes, we'll be finished in another 20 minutes. We will take the body to the morgue, and you two are free to go. We will need to process it and then you can have it sent to the funeral home. I'll stay in touch. Here's my card and a card for cleanup of the room once we've cleared the crime scene."

Sarabeth looks over at the other ambulance housing Rob's body. She starts to cry again. Wiping her tears from her face, she takes the cards from the detective.

"Thank you."

Debbie walks over to the ambulance. "Hey, Sar. How are you doing?

Sarabeth smiles at her friend. "I'm still so shaken. It's so much to take in, but I think we should get some food ready for everyone and do our last channeling. Will you help me with that? I'm worried about Sophia. Have you talked with her?"

"Yes, of course. I haven't talked to Sophia, but Jan has been in touch with Laurel. She said that Sophia is OK, and Laurel has been communicating with Rob's ghost. How do you want to tell her about what happened?"

"I don't know. I've been thinking about that. They need to take Lance to the hospital. That bullet needs to come out. So, after they leave, let's go get Sophia and see how to proceed."

The paramedic is watching Lance's vitals. "We need to go now," he says.

Sarabeth leans over and kisses Lance. He raises his hand to touch her face. "I'll see you soon, love." Sarabeth gets out of the back and stands with Debbie as the ambulance drives away. They walk over to the other ambulance.

"I need to see him," Sarabeth says.

The paramedic opens the door and turns.

"It might be difficult for you."

He unzips the black bag so that Sarabeth can see Rob's face.

Sarabeth goes through the back door toward Rob's body. She opens the bag further and looks at him. His skin is ashen, his eyes are closed, and his blond hair frames his face. She brushes his hair back and touches his cheek. Her eyes well with tears,

"Oh Rob, I'm so sorry." She looks at him for a long time.

Images of Sophia in his arms when she was small; palm trees blowing in the wind, sailing on the water together, and then the gun pointed at her, his eyes black, she jumps out of her reverie. She leans down and kisses his forehead. "Goodbye, my love." She looks at the paramedic and says, "Thank you. I'm finished."

Sarabeth exits the ambulance. She and Debbie walk toward the front door. "I'm going to text Laurel to bring in Sophia. I will talk with her. Can you get some food for everyone, then we can meet for the channeling, OK?"

The living room has mats laid out in a circle in place of chairs. Abby is standing in the center of the room. She directs Bob, Debbie, Jan, and Peter to choose a mat.

As they sit down, Abby says, "Sarabeth asked me to offer you each a healing to remove the discharge from today before she does the channeling. My work is more hands-on when I work with the angels in the higher dimensions of consciousness. I want you to lie down and take three deep cleansing breaths. I am going to place stones on you and work on each of you individually. Use the methods Sarabeth spoke of to lighten yourself and move into meditation."

Abby begins with Peter. She starts to choose stones. She pauses to listen to the inner direction from her guides. After placing stones on each person, she sits in the center of the four participants so she can touch each person while she listens to the inner guidance.

Laurel and Sarabeth are with Sophia in the kitchen. "Mom, I'm really sad about Dad. I like that Laurel said she can see dad and talk to him. I can kind of feel him too, but it's more like inside me than in my vision. Do you think I will hear Dad when I do the channeling? When is Lance coming back from the hospital?"

"I know you are. Me too. I'm glad you can feel him with you—that is very nice. The doctor said Lance has to stay the night. They said he lost a lot of blood, but he will be OK. How are you feeling about doing the channeling tonight? Do you want to go over how you open to the channel again?"

Sophia looks anxiously at her mom.

"Yes, let's talk about it again."

As Sophia starts to recite the opening procedure, Abby walks into the kitchen from the back of the living room. "We're ready for you, Sarabeth."

"Oh, OK. Laurel, let's go in with the group. You too, Sophia. I'll let you know when it's your turn."

They all enter the room and take places on the mats. Sarabeth sits down on the white couch. Her friends face her from their mats. "Thank you, Abby, for assisting everyone to shift their energy. Let's see if we can access more information about what happened and whatever the channel wants to share with us on this final day of the retreat. Please take three cleansing breaths."

"*Source energy, allow me to be a clear healing channel. I call in one hundred thousand angels to please come in and fill this room; I invite in only high frequency light beings. Please come in to guide me and offer me interpretation for this final evening of this retreat on healing psycho-emotional trauma through the ancient traditions... Thank you for your protection and guidance dear Archangel Michael, the Council of Twelve, Archangel Raphael, Mercury, Metatron, the Marys, Orion, and Sirius...*"

Sarabeth relaxes into her chair, feeling a deep love overwhelming her. She feels the voice and words from the channel. Her voice lightens and softens as she speaks the words, augmented by the complete knowing of what is being shared.

"*Dearly beloved, we are here for this final night together, and we want you to know how much we love each of you. We want to offer guidance on what has occurred today in your home, Sarabeth. Integration of spirit, mind, and body are necessary for healing and health. We have talked about how to increase your integration process, experience a sense of allowing. To be at peace within, go into your heart center and open to love. From an open heart center, you are able to receive a higher frequency of light. Anchor this in your field through intention and connection to source; you may imagine this as a light that moves through your chakra system and anchors into your field. Think of this as if you are stepping into the light, and the light pours in through and around you.*

"*Remember that attention and intention focus energy and creation...you create that to which you put your attention. Pay attention to that which brings you joy, that which you desire, and this is what you will create. You choose your creation through your attention and intention and the energy of love. Love promotes the blossoming of life; fear condenses and constricts. Fear cannot exist where there is love. To open to love, take in a deep breath and fill your lungs. As you exhale, feel the air moving through your body. Focus your attention on your heart space as you feel the pulsing there and the exchange of air in your lungs. Open your mind. Drop your attention from your thinking to your heart space. It is your feeling, but it is feeling informed by compassion and a sense of security in love. Come from your heart space and you will be in the energy of love, in the space of love. This energy allows for direct communication with spirit, compassion, and light.*

"*The energies of flow and allowing are key to increasing the frequency of light. Allowing each emotion its expression, with love and compassion, allows for it to be released and you to be guided to your true essential being. From this space you can see what is in your best interest, and out of a natural inner guidance, be guided by what brings you joy. The continuum of control and allowing is connected to creation and ownership in your life path.*

"*We discussed in previous channelings the importance of whole foods, fresh water, movement, daily meditation, and clean air, breath.*

And that both excess and insufficiency create dissonance in the balance within, dull the capacity for light, and lead to disease within each person.

"Today's interpretation focuses on how to incorporate the knowledge from your intuition and various timelines into your soul path. We see that this is most useful with respect to relationships, friendships, partnerships, and love relationships. In order to do this, you have to be willing to look underneath the driving force of fear and anger toward a higher purpose of your soul.

"Over the last two nights we spoke about how each soul has a relationship to a group, and often comes into incarnation with a set of agreements to fulfill. This is a layered process and includes what is called 'karma,' or karmic agreements. Most, but not all, of what drives a spirit-human are these soul agreements made prior to incarnation. There are different timeline dimensions and there are relationships from past and future lives, all of which affect what choices a being makes throughout her life. At its core, this is driven by the soul purpose of each spirit human. Each being may have some conscious knowledge of the agreements driving his or her decisions—or not. This is driven by the being's soul. The level of conscious awareness regarding these decisions is important in helping each spirit-human navigate the labyrinth of the inner knowing of each soul path.

"The opening to this is through the higher dimensions of consciousness. What blocks this path is getting stuck in third and fourth dimension. It pulls you into the space from which karma arises. Once you get into the fifth dimension you see that spirit is the powerful creator. You are made up of the tapestry of your and your ancestors' lives; it is woven in what you think of as your DNA. It directs you through emotion, your senses, what you feel as something subtle driving you toward a relationship or connection.

"We spoke in a previous channeling about the fifth dimension of consciousness. And the difference between intuition and ego-based drives in terms of how you experience them. Like the issue of attention and intention, your work is to assist yourself and others to focus on the intuition and release the ego-based drives. This appears to be difficult for humans, as the thing you need to release feels more intense and the thing you need to focus on is subtle. Living in third intensity 'feels' like

the thing to focus on, and so often as one is elevating their consciousness they get stuck in an intense cycle of patterning. We spoke of using
your heart center to help jump you out of that rut, as well as acupuncture points and other tools to help realign you to balance so you can
hear and listen to that inner soul voice. What happened here today
was this stuck patterning.

"Although you each have fifth-dimensional selves assisting you,
you have to be sufficiently open to these messages. This is why we
have offered so many tools to heal the body and mind to allow these
messages to enter through your chakra and meridian system. When
a spirit-human is blocked in his lower chakras the drives of fear and
anger block him from moving into fifth dimension when under stress.
This is especially true when karmic challenges are in play.

"The information we presented earlier are ways to help you as
you begin to feel the intensity so that you can focus your intention
and attention on your true soul's purpose. If one is blocked, he will feel
an inability to quiet his mind.

"To understand the power of the fifth dimension of healing you
have to be willing to accept that alignment with spirit and your spiritual path is a direct connection to source. You must let go of your mind
being in control and be at peace with the concept of one source of light.
The part that usually blocks this is attachment to mind, and the illusion of control, and the personality you call the ego.

"Rob became entangled in this struggle. He lost his sense of soul
self and was driven mad by the information he received through his
third dimensional rather than fifth dimensional patterning. Time
is all happening at once. It is like string theory from physics: many
happenings at the same time. The being has the ability to comprehend
between one and five happenings at a time. So, for those stuck in third
dimension, the idea of birth and death and linear time is the only
possible perception. As one opens to this idea, there are possibilities of
past lives and future lives along the linear continuum.

"The spirit-human evolution is happening multidimensionally.
This shift is ramping up and moving at a faster pace over the last year
and this will continue to take on speed. We see that Rob was on the

precipice of elevating his consciousness. He felt the intensity of the ramping energy on the planet and the intensity of his karmic cycle with Lance and Sarabeth. It became too much for him to bear because he hadn't practiced these tools we have been sharing. He understood them cognitively, but he had not yet incorporated them into his daily practice.

"We want to underscore that this is a powerful gift that Rob has offered you. Working in the light in third on the planet requires a deep recognition of how suffering and trauma teach us our soul lessons, but if one is unable to transform that suffering and trauma, he can be driven to act solely from secondary drives. The tools are not enough, and those who teach this information must be mindful of what can happen when one is not mindful of the mind and body of those you heal. There is miraculous healing, but this is in each spirit-human soul path. Do not push the river; focus on allowing and flow. Curves and turns are part of the river.

"This is why the metaphor of the labyrinth is the way in which we want you to consider your way through to evolution of your consciousness and that of your clients. To move through the labyrinth efficiently you need access to that quiet voice. The way this applies to your consciousness is how you have to develop your internal connection to your soul and listen to the subtle sensations and intuitions as you are interacting with others in relationship. Fear and ego-based drives can interfere with this. The walls of the labyrinth are those traumas and suffering, those ego-based drives.

"Begin to experience a deep connection with source in your everyday lives, bringing your connection and fifth-dimensional experiences into your everyday practices and lives. Focus on holding a connection to the divine feminine within you. You can do this through a direct connection with that aspect of the divine if you are already living in sixth or seventh dimension, as some of you are, or by way of connecting to an archetype who holds that nature, White Buffalo Woman, white or green Tara, Quan Yin, Mary, Shekinah, Mary Magdalene, Lady Nada, are some ascended masters or archetypes that hold this high level divine feminine energy. Earlier interpretations discussed that balance of yin with yang or masculine and feminine to

be the pivot point of the Tao. All these offerings are leading you toward balance or right action to remain on your soul path.

"Finally, we want to remind each of you that as you have enlightened yourselves toward your soul path in this retreat, there will be an integration process over the next four weeks. Each of you may have to face some revelation that creates a breaking off of old patterns that you didn't realize were holding you back. This may affect your relationships, and your relationship with yourself, and how your soul path is directing you. This may take you in directions you are surprised by. Be gentle with yourselves. We are here. We love you.

"Today we are not opening to questions...remember to drink plenty of water to assist your assimilation of this information at the cellular level as you are integrating this information and increasing the degree and frequency of light you are each holding; today it may be best to cleanse your energy field with asafetida and frankincense as well as salt and allow yourselves plenty of rest to help with assimilation of this information. Grounding foods will be essential. You may ground by walking on the earth or grass in your bare feet. Salt on the balls of your feet will assist to bring you into your bodies while simultaneously encouraging the anchoring of the light and new information. We are going to lighten the energy so that Sarabeth and Sophia can shift places."

Sarabeth gets up from the couch and walks over to Sophia.

"OK, kiddo, it's your turn. You can sit on the couch to face us."

Sophia gets up and walks to the couch. She sits down and crosses her feet underneath her.

Sophia quickly begins. She looks at her mom and then reaches for a lozenge. She closes her eyes again as she puts it in her mouth.

"OK," Sophia begins in her most urgent yet respectful voice, "I am open to receiving the information from Liu Ruyi to explain about Liu Ruyi's death, my connection to him and Peter, and the writing that was stolen so many years ago; the events I saw in my dream."

Sophia quiets her mind and takes three cleansing breaths. She listens. Suddenly she feels her heart expand and sees the universe in her mind. She feels like she is floating in the stars. She begins to speak.

"Dear, sweet Sophia, it is always a pleasure to communicate with you. Your spirit is such a delight for us and you are such a bright light on the planet. We send you so much love and light. Liu Ruyi is here to help you share the work you saw in you dream.

Sophia's voice changes as she speaks, it lightens and softens.

You were given the dream to begin your search about your heritage. Your spark carries the full information about the writing that was stolen. This information is necessary for the upleveling of the human race. It is about light, love, and oneness. My father loved Confucianism, and I too feel the importance of knowing the right timing for all things. However, you carry within you the ability to create miracles instantaneously. It is through the genuine living in the intuitive and sensing world together connected by the light of spirit. When you are at play and not thinking, you do this. You create. As soon as you let your mind lead, you lose the higher frequency and drop to the level of humanity now.

"The dream was a seed for you to begin to move into the perfection of living in your spirit-guided, intuitive-sensing self. Sophia, I see you, Sarabeth, Lance, Peter, and Jan re-creating this work on the planet. Jan, you have already seen the importance of using the five spirits and their points in a spiral fashion. We are offering this information for you to develop another pattern of how to create energy alchemy.

"You accurately understand that what you saw was a spiral. Using the power of the five-three-one of gathering medicine and starting in the navel chakra, at ren 8 moving the energy up and out to ren 12, then spiraling to the left at stomach 25, moving down and inward to ren 3, then continuing through the dan mien and downward to du 1, connecting to ren 1, you activate inner energy force. Concentrate on your breath while you are focusing on the spiral of energy. Breathing in for a count of four, holding at the top of the breath for a count of

four, and then exhaling for a count of four. This offers a way to recon-
nect with the inner divine feminine. By calling on Archangel Gabriel
and meditating with the violet flame, you can feel this energy growing
and spiraling through you. This is Energy Alchemy. The connection to
the labyrinth discussed in earlier dialogues offers a structure so you
can open to your inner subconscious and a spiritual journey to the
center of your soul. These points connect with your fifth dimensional
blueprint and soul plan. This is most effective if you also use toning
bowls and burn copal over the points.

"I must go now. Be at peace, Sophia. This is a huge responsibility,
but it is also a gift and an adventure. Know that your mother and your
dear friends here have set a path for you to follow. Although you are a
leader, you are not alone. I am always here for you. You may always
call on me through this process when you need my support. So much
love to you, dear."

Sophia opens her eyes and looks at Sarabeth.

"So now I thank everyone, right, Mom?"

Sarabeth gently wipes tears from her eyes.

"Yes, dear, that is the next step; you are doing well."

"OK, thank you everyone—Archangel Michael and all
the high light beings for your support and your information
today. Thank you, Liu Ruyi."

Sarabeth looks at Sophia and says, "Archangel Michael,
if you could clear the energy, thank you, thank you.
Kadosh, kadosh, kadosh. Om mani padme hum. Om, gam,
Ganapataye, namaha. Gate, gate, paragate, parasamgate,
Bodhi, svaha! Om shanti, shanti, shanti."

ABOUT THE AUTHOR

Dr. Beth Gineris is an author, intuitive healer, psychologist, and practitioner of energetic medicine who has treated patients clinically for over 20 years. As an author, she has produced articles across the internet and two nonfiction books: *Turning NO to ON: The Art of Parenting with Mindfulness*, and *Turning ME to WE: The Art of Partnering with Mindfulness*

Dr. Gineris educates an international following on the techniques of living a powerful, wholistic life grounded in wellness and mindfulness. Her work integrates alternative healing techniques—including acupuncture, yoga and energetic medicine, and intuitive counseling—with her academic training. She has master's degrees in counseling, Chinese medicine, and business administration. She also holds a PhD. in Applied Eco-Psychology.

Sarabeth and The Five Spirits is her first work of fiction.

ABOUT THE PUBLISHER

The Sager Group was founded in 1984. In 2012, it was chartered as a multimedia content brand, with the intention of empowering those who create art—an umbrella beneath which makers can pursue, and profit from, their craft directly, without gatekeepers. TSG publishes books; ministers to artists and provides modest grants; designs logos, products and packaging, and produces documentary, feature, and commercial films. By harnessing the means of production, The Sager Group helps artists help themselves. For more information, visit TheSagerGroup.net

MORE BOOKS FROM THE SAGER GROUP

#MeAsWell, A Novel
by Peter Mehlman

The Orphan's Daughter, A Novel
by Jan Cherubin

*Meeting Mozart: A Novel Drawn from the Secret Diaries
of Lorenzo Da Ponte*
by Howard Jay Smith

The Allergic Boy Versus the Left-Handed Girl: A Novel
by Michael Kun

Eat Wheaties! A Novel
By Michael Kun

Miss Havilland, A Novel
by Gay Daly

*Shaman: The Mysterious Life and Impeccable Death
of Carlos Castaneda*
by Mike Sager

Lifeboat No. 8: Surviving the Titanic
by Elizabeth Kaye

See our entire library at TheSagerGroup.net

THE SAGER GROUP

Artifex Te Adiuva

Made in the USA
Middletown, DE
28 December 2021

57252356R00135